China on the Way

中国进行时

刘东平 瞿淑蓉 编著
高松 陈春勇 王欢 韩清月 郭辉 翻译

华语教学出版社
SINOLINGUA

First Edition 2007

Second Printing 2008

ISBN 978-7-80200-389-7

Copyright 2007 by Sinolingua

Published by Sinolingua

24 Baiwanzhuang Road, Beijing 100037, China

Tel: (86)10-68320585

Fax: (86)10-68326333

http://www.sinolingua.com.cn

E-mail: hyjx@sinolingua.com.cn

Printed by Beijing Foreign Languages Printing House

Distributed by China International Book Trading Corporation

35 Chegongzhuang Xilu, P.O. Box 399

Beijing 100044, China

Printed in the People's Republic of China

前　言

2008年北京奥运会和2010年上海世博会日益临近，中国正在成为世界公众的关注点和国际媒体的聚焦点，"中国热"正方兴未艾，这一切都为中国国家形象的塑造提供了千载难逢的机遇。

的确，有不少外国人会对中国产生一些疑问：为什么中国经济会突飞猛进？为什么中国会出现姚明那样的NBA篮球明星？中国会不会把全球的石油用光？中国有朝一日会不会在经济实力上超过美国……这当中有好奇、羡慕，也夹杂着猜疑与不安。中国的形象也因此变得更加复杂、多元和丰富。中国，再也无法用一个非好即坏的标尺来判定了。

可以说，一百个人，有一百个人眼中的中国，他们对正在发展的中国充满了兴趣，他们渴望用自己的眼睛去观察，去体会；用自己的头脑去判断，去思考。

本书就可以帮助你阅读、认识和判别，就像本书封面的眼睛一样。

这双眼睛，好像万花筒，带你去捕捉今天中国五彩缤纷的生活，日新月异的变化。

这双眼睛，好像导航员，引你透过一些普通中国人的生活经历和想法，去了解今天中国经济正在腾飞的一个个侧面、一个个领域。

这双眼睛充满诚意，它传达了中国人的友善、好客和满腔热忱；这双眼睛并不遮掩，它把中国的发展、变化、传统、现实、问题和苦恼浓缩成一个个色彩斑斓的场景，让更多的人看到一个发展中的中国……

Preface

As the 2008 Beijing Olympic Games and the 2010 Shanghai World EXPO are approaching, China has come into the spotlight of both the people and the media from all over the world, and the world seems to have caught China fever. This provides China with a unique opportunity to build up its image.

Understandably, quite a few foreigners have questions concerning China. For instance: why is China's economy developing so fast? How did China come up with a NBA basketball star like Yao Ming? Will China use up the world's oil supplies? Will China overtake the United States some day in terms of economic power?... Such questions imply curiosity, envy, as well as doubts and worries, resulting in an even more complicated, multi-faceted and profound image of a China that can no longer be judged as either being good or bad.

It is safe to say that among a hundred people there are a hundred different views on China. They are all fascinated by China, eager to observe China with their own eyes and draw their own conclusions.

This book aims at assisting you in reading, learning and judging, as is reflected by the eye on the cover.

These eyes are like a kaleidoscope, showing you China's colorful life and the exciting changes that take place every day.

These eyes are like a navigator, leading you through experiences and thoughts of ordinary Chinese so that you can learn about every aspect of today's China with its booming economy.

These eyes are honest, reflecting the friendliness, hospitality and enthusiasm of the Chinese people. And these eyes never attempt to look away from anything. On the contrary, they have captured the developments, the changes, the traditions, the reality, the problems and the sorrows in a series of colorful pictures, to show a China that is still developing....

目 录 Contents

◎ 第一篇 生活与时尚　Life & Fashion

◎ 第二篇 文化与符号　Culture & Symbol

◎ **第三篇 社会与发展 Society & Development**

第一篇

生活与时尚

LIFE & FASHION

胖——已不再是福

　　宽宽是北京的一名11岁小学生，身高4.9英尺，体重130多磅。他爬楼梯呼哧带喘，体育课项目也常不及格。为了减肥，宽宽参加了一家减肥俱乐部的减肥训练，与他一同减肥的还有20多名小胖子。

　　像宽宽这样的肥胖青少年在中国越来越多。据一项统计显示：目前中国的肥胖者数量已远远超过

9000万，超重者高达2亿。肥胖儿童的数量也在近15年间增长了28倍以上。

医学专家认为，生活的富足，食用高热量、高脂肪美食的无节制，过多地乘坐汽车，缺少运动，以及长时间保持坐姿等生活方式是造成中国肥胖者队伍悄然壮大的主要因素。

中国医学科学院的武阳丰教授说："中国曾是拥有最瘦人群的国家之一，如今中国的肥胖人群正在迅速赶上西方国家，而这一切是在很短时间内发生的。"

肥胖队伍的迅速壮大，一方面反映了中国人的生活越来越富足、舒适了，而另一方面也提醒人们要养成健康的生活习惯。肥胖带来的健康问题已愈来愈引起中国社会各方面的广泛关注。专家们呼吁，要改变不良生活方式，控制膳食热量和脂肪摄入量，增加体力活动和体育锻炼，这样才能有效削减和抑制肥胖人群的增长。

Being Fat —— No Longer Bliss

Kuankuan, an 11-year-old pupil in Beijing, is 4.9 feet high and weighs over 130 pounds. He often fails his P.E. tests at school, and would even become out of breath when climbing the stairs. In order to lose weight, he has registered for a program in a Weight-loss Club

along with twenty other obese children.

Nowadays, China has more and more obese adolescents like Kuankuan. Statistics shows that at present, the number of obese people in China has far exceeded 90 million, while the number of overweight people has reached 200 million. The number of obese children has increased by 28 times over the past 15 years.

Medical experts believe that the dramatic increase in the prevalence of obesity in China is mainly caused by an unhealthy lifestyle, including the increasing availability of labor saving appliances, indulgence in foods with high calorie and fatty content, overuse of automobiles, lack of physical activities, and remaining in a sitting position for long periods of time.

Professor Wu Yangfeng of Chinese Academy of Medical Sciences commented: "China used to be a country with the thinnest people. However, within a very short period of time, China's obese population is quickly catching up with that of developed countries."

The rapid increase in obesity would then seem to be the result of an on-going change in the lifestyle of Chinese people whose lives are becoming more and more affluent and comfortable. At the same time, health problems caused by obesity have called great attention of all aspects of Chinese society. Experts advocate that people should correct their unhealthy lifestyles, eat less, eat more healthy foods, and get more exercise. Only by doing these may the obesity problem be effectively controlled and even reduced. However, while diet, medical treatment, and physical activities may

be a solution for the already overweight and obese, it is most important for children and adolescents to develop healthy lifestyles and behaviors from an early age.

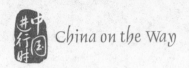
吃面包还是吃馒头

　　漫步中国都市的街头，你不时地会发现装修精美的面包店。中国北方人曾给人偏爱吃馒头、包子等面食的印象，而现在这种习惯正被逐渐改变。如今西式的面包店越开越多，相比之下，卖馒头、包子的店铺却难觅踪迹了。

　　在一些新崛起的中产阶层看来，面包专卖店的

繁盛，已成为大都市的一道靓丽的"国际化风景"。据了解，北京市政府计划在2008年奥运会前，让西餐业翻番。奥运会和国际化，让喜爱面包文化的人士更为理直气壮。

面包成为流行，主人翁是城里的年轻人和新中产阶层。在一家面包店里，一对年轻情侣正悠然品尝着面包。女孩儿说，虽自小吃中式主食，但西方饮食却是她的偏爱，她喜欢面包被咬在口中那种软软的、香香的感觉。从中式到西式的口味转换，她没感觉任何不适。至于价钱，她的男友说："这在我们承受的范围内。"

北京清华大学东门附近，新开张的一家面包店成了大学生的休闲好去处。下课后，三三两两的年轻人来到这里，要一杯香浓的咖啡，手捧精致的西式小甜点，优雅地和朋友聊着天，自然、惬意。

人们也因此从过去偏爱热闹、喧哗，逐渐转变为现在的个人化、安静、悠闲和注重隐私。

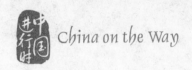

　　不过对一般市民来说，时髦的面包店有时让他们不适应。35岁的谢丽说，她很少踏进面包店，因为面包太贵了，也不习惯天天把面包当主食吃。她的同事、朋友中也有不少人仍从超市里买馒头、包子、花卷、豆沙包、烙饼等中式面食回家吃；而精美的面包仅作为早餐和点心，成为更多中国人的选择。这也是中国接纳外国饮食习惯的一种体现吧。

Western Bread or Chinese One?

Bakeries are sprouting up in cities across China, both in the south and in the north. For northern residents, steamed bread and stuffed buns are considered a traditional staple, but nowadays, this preference is not as strong. To cater to this new trend, shops selling Western-flavored cakes and breads are growing in popularity. Some say this is a sign of China's prosperity and modernization.

To many of the new middle class, flourishing bakeries are symbols of major cities becoming more international. One result of this perception may be seen in Beijing's plans to double its Western cuisine sector by the 2008 Olympiad. The international nature of the sports event and growing trends towards internationalization add more justice to those dedicated to spreading the bread culture.

Young urbanites and the middle class are patrons of bakeries. At a bakery, two college sweethearts are enjoying their delicacies.

Though her staple diet has been Chinese food since childhood, the girl loves Western cuisine. She finds it quite natural to change from Chinese to Western style breads. When asked about the cost, her boyfriend replies, "We can afford it."

A new bakery by the east gate of Tsinghua University in Beijing has become a hangout for students. From noisy restaurants to quiet privacy, many Chinese are changing their way of dining under Western influence.

But for ordinary residents, the flashily decorated bakeries are somewhat too dazzling. Xie Li, 35, is a window-shopper of sponge cakes. She seldom steps into the shops as the wares are too expensive. Her colleagues and friends often buy more traditional steamed bread, stuffed buns, twisted rolls and baked pancakes from supermarkets, rather than loaf breads, while young patrons savor their breads and chat in the bakeries.

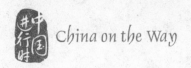

中国孩子"上班"忙

　　望子成龙，望女成凤，是中国人传统的育子观念。尤其在今天的中国，大部分家庭都是独生子女，而社会竞争却日益激烈。家长们于是把子女教育摆在重中之重的位置，从小抓起，舍得投入。这就出现了一个"有趣"而普遍的社会现象：孩子们"上班"

忙，家长们"花钱"忙。

中国一家研究咨询机构最新发布的对城市普通居民家庭的调查数据显示：在所调查的北京、上海、广州、武汉、长沙、西安、成都、哈尔滨等八个城市的家庭中，4～12岁的儿童，半数以上都在课堂之外上各种特长班或兴趣班；有12岁以下"上班"儿童的家庭，平均每月用于孩子"上班"的费用约为200元。北京和上海等大城市的花费还要高。

在"上班"的孩子们中，48.9%的孩子每周需要花1～2小时"上班"，33.8%的孩子需要花3～5小时。每周"上班"时间超过6小时的孩子比例达到了17.3%。这些时间仅仅是指在"班上"所花的时间，不包括孩子奔波在"上下班"路上所需要的时间，以及"下班"后所需要的各种复习、练习时间。

调查显示，孩子们所上的"班"种类繁多，从最普及的英语班（63.9%），到很平常的绘画班（25%）、舞蹈班（18.7%），从钢琴、小提琴、二胡、琵琶等各种中西乐器班（10.1%），到奥数班（8.4%）、跆拳道、散打、武术班（5.3%），还有游泳班、思维训练班、写作班、围棋班……五花八门，应有尽有。

调查还发现，让孩子"上班"的家长们大致可以分成以下几种类型：一是未雨绸缪型家长，这类型家长占家长调查人数的37.7%。他们认为未来社会竞争激烈，多学点东西有助于提升孩子未来的竞争力；

二是能力培养型家长，占23.9%。他们感到有必要培养孩子的文化艺术修养，提高孩子的个人素质；三是满足兴趣型家长，占10.5%。他们看到孩子对某方面有兴趣或有所长，于是因势利导，既满足了孩子兴趣，又学到一门知识或

技艺；四是被动跟风型家长，此类家长有17.4%。他们看到周围的孩子都在上"班"，深感自家孩子不上不行，不能让孩子输在起跑线上，于是随大流，盲目地给孩子报班；五是注重社会交往型家长，占5.8%。他们觉得独生子女家庭的孩子社会交往面狭窄，应让孩子多接触社会，培养孩子与人交往的能力；另外还有"子承父业"型家长，占4.8%，他们本人对某些方面有爱好，希望通过培养子女来实现自己的梦想。

不仅国内孩子"上班"忙，海外的华人父母也普遍重视子女教育，对子女们要求极为严格。曾在伦敦一家中文学校补习中文的华裔女孩这样说："从小学开始，父母便要我做课外练习，每天要完成不少功

课呢。"

英国教育部曾公布了一项对各民族学生表现的统计数据，华裔学生的成绩名列第一。其实，并非海外华裔子女特别聪明过人，而是中国人勤奋刻苦的优良传统，不断地通过这些华裔父母和子女表现出来。

Chinese Kids—
Busy Attending Classes All Day Long

It is a tradition for all Chinese parents to raise their children to be a "somebody" and long to see their children succeed in life. Particularly in modern times, as most families have but one child and competition has become more and more fierce in the society, parents give high priority to their children's education, investing large amounts of money in education from a very early age. Consequently, there appears an interesting yet common phenomenon as the children hurry to attend classes of all kinds, and their parents hurry to spend money on them.

According to the latest statistics in a survey on ordinary city dwellers conducted by a Chinese research and consulting organization, of all the families polled in the cities of Beijing, Shanghai, Guangzhou, Wuhan, Changsha, Xi'an, Chengdu, and Harbin, half of the children aged from 4 to 12 have attended specialty classes or interest classes in their spare time; families with a child below 12 years of age spend on average 200 yuan per month on the classes

their children attend. Families in big cities like Beijing and Shanghai spend even more.

Of all the kids attending these classes, 48.9% spend 1-2 hours per week on the classes, 33.8% spend 3-5 hours, and 17.3% spend 6 hours or more. The time mentioned above merely refers to the actual time they spend in class, excluding the time spent in transporting to and from the classes and in after class study.

Surveys indicate that the classes the children attend vary from the most popular English classes (63.9%) to drawing (25%), dancing (18.7%), Chinese and Western music classes including piano, violin, erhu, pipa, etc. (10.1%), International Math Olympiad (8.4%), martial arts (5.3%), as well as swimming, logical-thinking trainings, writings, and Go, a classic board game.

The surveys also find that parents who have their children attend these classes roughly fall into the following six groups: The first includes the pre-emptive parents (37.7%), who believe that as competition becomes increasingly intense, it is helpful for their children to get as much knowledge as they can so as to become more competitive for the future. The second group is made up of parents who care more their children's capability (23.9%). They find it favorable to develop the cultural and artistic attainments of their children and raise their personal quality. The third group includes parents who care more their children's interest (10.5%) who notice in their children certain interest or talent and thus encourage them to develop by enrolling them in classes, which not only caters for their interest, but also expands their knowledge or skills. The fourth

group includes passively imitating parents (17.4%), who see children of other families attending classes of this kind or that, and just follow suit, believing that their children should not fall behind their peers at the very beginning. The fifth group consists of parents who emphasize social intercourse (5.8%). In their opinion, nowadays, as the only child of the family, their children tend to have a more sheltered life. Therefore, enrollment in classes becomes necessary to help their children develop their social and communications skills. The last group of parents consists of those who want their children to develop certain specialties according to the will of the parents (4.8%). They themselves have some hobbies in certain areas and they pin the hope of realizing their dreams and hobbies on their children.

However, this phenomenon occurs not only within China. As a matter of fact, Chinese people living overseas attach much significance to the education of their children as well. They are often quite strict with their children in terms of studies. A Chinese girl attending Chinese class at a school in London confessed: "Ever since my primary school, I have been required by my parents to attend extra-curricular classes. I have to deal with mountains of homework every day."

According to the statistics from the Department for Children, Schools and Families in the UK concerning the performance of students of all ethnic groups, Chinese children take first place. This does not mean that Chinese children outsmart their foreign peers. As a matter of fact, their excellent performances have best illustrated the fine Chinese tradition which emphasizes diligence.

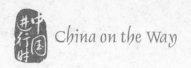
城市人的心爱宠物

　　如今，随着中国经济的发展，人民生活水平的提高，养宠物之风在城市的普通家庭中日渐流行。每到夏日傍晚，在居民小区、人行便道、街心花园绿地，都能看到那些悠闲的遛狗人，假日郊游的家庭轿车

里，也能看到端坐的宠物猫、宠物狗的身影。许多国外纯种名犬、名猫已经走进了中国普通人的家庭。

宠物是善解人意、充满智慧的小精灵，它们与人类的感情纯真而美好。据调查，伴侣动物对人的身心健康有直接或间接的影响，它可以成为家人之间交流的纽带，或陌生人之间最轻松的话题。特别是老年人，他们所需要的安全感、价值感、被爱和被需要的感觉，伴侣动物都可以为之提供。与宠物为伴的孩子，也更富有爱心和同情心。

走进遍布城市各个角落的宠物商店，你可以看到，现在宠物用品几乎和人类的差不多了，不但有宠物衣服、雨衣、背包、玩具，还有营养保健品（钙片等）、美发剂、洗眼液、滴耳露、沐浴液、香水等，整个宠物商店琳琅满目，应有尽有。

时下，许多城市人把宠物当孩子来养，对宠物的服务要求也越来越精细了，因而带动了宠物产业的快速发展。在一些宠物美容商店里，宠物可以享受到无微不至的服务。比如，宠物美容师可以给狗提供包括洗澡、吹干、掏耳朵、剪指甲、修理脚底毛和肛毛、修形等全套护理服务，一般费用是几十元到二三百元。收费多少主要跟狗的大小、毛长短有关。还有一些狗必须定期来修形，如贵妇、雪娜瑞等。宠物美容院还可以为一些名贵宠物做出100多种发型，但价钱也的确不菲，一般一次要百八十元。据说在北京、上

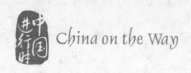
海等大城市，宠物产业的市场销售额已达20亿元。

　　但城市的养宠物热也带来了一些社会问题，如社区内的宠物猫狗惊吓了孩子、骚扰了居民，这该如何教育和管理？街上的流浪狗、流浪猫多起来，怎么收养和看护它们？宠物们在公园绿地上大小便，污染了环境……这些问题正在日益引起城市管理者和公众的关注。除了政府有关部门制定和发布一些小动物管理条令外，一些城市还成立了保护小动物协会，不少民间热心人士也积极行动起来，收留养护流浪猫狗，并通过宣传来提高人们"养宠物要注重环保"的意识。相信未来中国人会更文明、更理性地饲养宠物，动物和人类会更和谐地相处。

Pets Adored by City Dwellers

With the recent development of economy and the improvement of people's living standards in China, more and more ordinary households in cities have started raising pets. At dusk on a summer day, you can always see people leisurely walking their dogs in the neighborhood, the walkways and the grassy central parks. Pet cats and dogs are also seen sitting in the family cars during holiday travels. Exotic purebred dogs and cats are more and more often being raised in ordinary Chinese households.

Pets are like considerate and smart fairies, friendly and honest

to human beings. Pets have an influence on people's physical or mental health, they can be the bridge between family members or a comfortable topic of conversation between strangers. This is especially the case for elderly people, for whom pets can provide a sense of security, value, being loved and being needed. Children who make friends with pets tend to be more loving and sympathetic as well.

Stepping into pet shops scattered over every corner of a city, you can find various pet goods which are very similar to those in shops for human consumers. The great variety of goods including pet clothes, rain clothes, rucksacks, toys, nutritional supplements, shampoo, eye washes, ear drops, body lotion, perfume... pack the shops from wall to wall.

Nowadays, many people raise pets as their own children, thus becoming ever more discerning in the services provided for their pets. This in turn drives the quick development of the pet industry. Some beauty salons for pets provide a variety of meticulous services. For example, the pet beautician can provide a grooming package of services for pet dogs including bathing, drying, picking ears, trimming nails, tidying the hair on the soles and the rump, etc. The prices for these services vary with the size of the dog and the length of the hair, ranging from below a hundred to hundreds yuan. Some breeds of dogs such as Poodles and Schnauzers need to be trimmed regularly. Some salons can even do more than a hundred hairstyles for dogs which may cost a hundred yuan or so. It is said that in big cities like Beijing and Shanghai, the pet industry generates a revenue of two billion yuan.

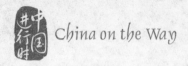

However, the mania for raising pets has also brought some social problems. For instance, how to deal with the pet dogs and cats in the community who have scared the children and disturbed the residents? How to protect and look after the increasing number of homeless dogs and cats? What about pets answering the nature's call in the public places? Problems like these are becoming more of a concern for city managers and the general public. Apart from regulations regarding the management of pets, some cities have set up committees for animal protection. Quite a few civilians have set out spontaneously to adopt and take care of homeless cats and dogs, and to strengthen public awareness of "being environment-friendly when raising pets" by way of advocacy. It is firmly believed that in the near future, Chinese will raise pets in a more civilized and rational way and that animals and human beings can live in harmony with each other.

还想再买一辆车

20多年前，走在中国的城市街区，你会发现骑自行车上班的车队川流不息，茫茫如海，所以外国人形象地称中国为"自行车的海洋、自行车王国"。而今，中国已跨入汽车时代，家庭轿车的数量超过2000万辆，年增长率超过80%。

不知不觉中，不少人发现身边拥有两辆轿车的家庭越来越多。据权威调查机构数据显示，钱袋越来越鼓的中国家庭正在步入一个购买第二辆车的高峰，2010年前后，中国中等收入家庭将普遍拥有一辆或

多辆轿车。

张女士就是一位准备购买"第二辆车"的消费者。她说，几年前购买的奥拓车早就不够用了，自从孩子出生后，他们夫妻俩就有了换车的念头。而近一两年中档车已经大幅降价，性价比非常高，因此他们准备添买一辆11万左右的爱丽舍。

私家车主颜先生最近也想专为妻子买一辆新车。他说："我原有一辆20多万的中高级商务车，由于工作很忙，妻子和孩子上班、上学还得靠公交车或打车。但现在养两辆车对我家不是什么问题了，所以我就想再买一辆10万元左右的轿车，让妻子上班开，还可以接送孩子。"

中国权威汽车调查咨询机构新华信公司发布最新调查结果称，44.4%的被调查者把拥有汽车视为

改变生活质量的重要标志，有40.3%的被调查者认为车辆在使用到第五年时为最佳的换车时机，有半数以上被调查者说他们最愿意购买的是10万元左右、经济实用的家庭轿车。这些数字表明，中国家庭购买"第二辆车"的热潮正方兴未艾。

I Want to Buy Another Car

As recently as two decades ago, if you walked on the streets in China, you would have seen a sea of people going to work by bicycle in an endless stream. Therefore, foreigners regarded China the "Sea of Bicycles" or the "Kingdom of Bicycles". Now people are experiencing a flood of cars in this Chinese age of the automobile. The number of family cars has exceeded 20 million with an annual growth rate exceeding 80%.

Seemingly overnight, the number of Chinese families owning two cars has increased dramatically. Statistics from an authoritative investigatory apparatus show that many Chinese families seeing an increase of income level are contributing to an increase in the number of two-car-families. Speculation is that in 2010 or so, middle-income Chinese families will each have one or more cars.

Ms. Zhang, who was shopping for a second car, said that the small car branded Alto she bought several years ago was not enough for her family. Since her baby was born, she and her husband have

decided to buy another car. In recent years, medium-grade cars with a creditable performance have been sold at greatly reduced prices. This has made it possible for Ms. Zhang's family to buy their second car, an Elysee, worth some 110,000 yuan.

Recently, Mr. Yan, a private car owner who decided to buy a new car for his wife, said, "I have a medium to high-grade business car worth over 200,000 yuan. I am busy at work, and my wife and child go to work or school by bus or taxi. Now I can afford two cars, I will buy another worth about 100,000 yuan so that my wife can go to work and send our child to school by car."

According to the latest findings from Sinotrust Marketing Research and Consulting, reputable car investigatory and advisory body, 44.4% of the subjects of investigation view the owning of a car as an important tool to improve the quality of life, 40.3% of them hold the opinion that the best option for buying a second new car is when the old one has been used about five years, and more than half maintain that they would most readily buy utility family cars worth 100,000 yuan each. These figures show that the number of two-car Chinese families is just beginning to rise.

中国人的住宅梦

　　王东是一位从山东来北京外企工作的白领。刚开始工作时他一直是租房住，两年后他开始着手选购将属于自己的房子。经过了四处搜房、筹集房资和看房的种种辛苦后，他如愿在北京买下了一套100多平方米的新居。接下来他又开始了为装修而四处奔波的日子，虽辛苦却乐在其中。今天，在中国的

大都市里，像王东这样拥有较高文化素养和较好工作的年轻人很多，他们都在为拥有自己的住宅加倍努力！

改革开放后近20年来，中国逐渐实行了住宅商品化、货币化，原来由单位分配的住房皆转为货币补贴，由职工个人购买了，同时大量商品房、经济适用房等新住宅推向市场。

随着人们收入的不断增加和生活水平的提高，越来越多的人实现了他们的住宅梦。据统计，目前中国内地的城市人均住宅面积达到了26平方米，比1980年中国城镇居民人均住房面积增加了5倍多。许多北京人在京郊贷款买下了宽敞的新房，把市内的老房用来出租还贷。不少人还拥有了多套房产。

由于人们改善居住环境的需求不断加大，使得中国一些大中城市的房价迅速攀升，居高不下，令许多人"望房兴叹"。有不少年轻人为了买房，不得不向父母、亲友求援。有的人虽然住上了新房，也被沉重的房贷压成了"房奴"一族。

目前政府正在采取措施，逐渐规范管理房地产市场，如扩大中小户型住宅房比例，建设许多价格低廉的经济适用房、限价房和廉租房，以切实解决一些中低收入家庭的住房问题。

The Dream of Chinese
of Buying Their Own Houses

Wang Dong, a young man from Shandong Province, is an employee in a foreign enterprise in Beijing. After two years renting an apartment, he considered buying his own house. Despite great difficulties searching for a house and financing the payment, he eventually realized his dream of buying a new house of about 100 square meters in Beijing. The following days saw him busy with the furniture and decorations in the house. Tired as he was, he enjoyed it very much. Nowadays, in the metropolis, there are many young people like Wang Dong with higher education and decent jobs working hard for their dreams of buying their own houses.

In the past two decades after the implementation of the

reform and opening-up policy, China has phased in commercialized houses. The previous way of allocating houses to employees by their employers has been replaced by a new system of providing employees monetary subsidies to buy their own houses. Meanwhile, large numbers of commercial houses and economical apartments may also be traded on the market.

With the constant rise in people's income and living standards, more and more people have realized their dreams of buying their own houses. Statistics indicate that presently, the urbanites' per capita housing floor space is 26 square meters; an increase of more than 5 times compared to that of the year 1980. Many Beijingers choose to buy a spacious house in the suburbs on hire purchase and pay the loan with the income from renting out their old houses in downtown Beijing. Quite a few people have more than one house, even own luxury villa, especially those with high income such as actors, lawyers, and those on corporate management. In order that lower-income families may also enjoy house ownership, the government has built many cheap economical apartments and renting houses.

In recent years, sky-rocketing prices of houses in large and middle-sized cities have thwarted the efforts of many people who are longing for their own houses. In their quest to own a house, many young people use up all of their savings, and are compelled to seek financial help from their parents, relatives and friends. Although they at long last move into new houses, they must then bear the heavy burden of installed payment. They are even mocked as "house slaves". Fortunately, the government is taking some

measures such as building fixed-price houses and increasing the proportion of the medium and small-sized houses, in an effort to regulate the real estate market.

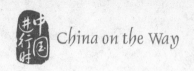
中国人的金钱观：
从攒钱到投资

　　"恭喜发财"，是过年时中国人见面常说的一句问候语，许多人还把印有"恭喜发财"四个烫金大字的对联贴在门上。

　　从古至今，中国人就有善于赚钱、攒钱的传统习惯。全球华商约6000万人，分布在170余个国家，靠辛勤劳作、经营积聚了大量财富和可观的金钱资本。在近年来中国引进的外国资本中，就有70%的资金直接来自于海外华商。

　　在中国，每当人们手中有了钱，会习惯性地把它先存进银行，以备急用之需。有时哪怕明天就要用钱，今天也要把钱存起来。中国人民银行曾进行过一次问卷调查，有33.4%的被调查者表示他们选择把余钱存进银行。另据统计，2005年中国个人存款约占家庭收入的30%。尽管随着经济发展，中国年轻人

的消费热潮高涨，但储蓄仍是普通家庭主要的理财方式。

而近一两年，这种情形发生了很大变化。人们的投资意识越来越浓，特别是在股票和基金牛市当道、收益率连创新高的刺激下，居民们对投资基金、股票的热情空前高涨。大量银行存款源源流向股市、基市，即使各大银行推出了国债、黄金、人民币和外汇理财等上百种产品，基金和股票仍然是最热门的投资品种。2007年第一季度，人民币Ａ股新开户数为500多万户，比2006年全年新增开户数还多近200万户，同年一季度，通过购买基金和股票流入股市的资金达到数千亿元之多。银行代理基金销售的柜台前常出现人满为患的景象。

中国证券业内人士说，随着中国居民对理财产品认知度的加深，特别是受股票、基金等收益较高的金融理财产品的影响，中国居民的金融投资意识会越来越强。

中国家庭资产结构也正发生深刻的变化。据专家分析，继股市、债市、期市、邮市、房产、保险投资之后，黄金有望成为中国百姓下一个重要的投资渠道。除此之外，古玩、字画、艺术品的投资收藏也成为一部分中国人的理财方式。

Chinese View on Money:
from Saving to Investing

In China, "Gong Xi Fa Cai (wish you a good fortune)" is a traditional greeting on Lunar New Year's Day. Many people also put up couplets with four big gilded characters "Gong Xi Fa Cai" on the door.

Ever since ancient times, Chinese people have been famous for being good at making money as well as saving money. Now, there are altogether 60 million Chinese businessmen in more than 170 countries throughout the world. Through hard work, they have accumulated a great amount of fortune and capital. Of all the foreign capital China has seen in recent years, seventy percent comes directly from these overseas Chinese businessmen.

In China, once people have extra money, they are used to saving it in the bank for emergencies. In some cases, even though they will use the money the next day, they deposit it in the bank today. According to a survey conducted by the People's Bank of China, 33.4% of the respondents preferred to save their money. Other statistics shows that a few years ago, Chinese people deposited about 30% of their total household income into banks. Even in a growing economy with younger Chinese increasingly active in consuming, saving still remains the major trend.

However, in recent years things have greatly changed. Chinese people become more and more interested in investing. Given the facts that the stock market and fund market are constantly on the rise, and giving investors ever-increasing yields, it is no surprise that people have shown great enthusiasm about investment in stocks and funds. Large amounts of bank deposits flow continuously to the stock and fund market. Although many major banks have put forward more than 100 kinds of financial products, such as government bonds, gold, domestic money and foreign exchanges, etc., funds and stocks are still the most popular choices for investment. In the first quarter of 2007 alone, there have been more than 5 million new accounts for Renminbi listing A-board, 2 million more than the overall new accounts opened during all of 2006. During the same period, hundreds of billions of Renminbi went to the stock market buying stocks and funds. Those banks acting as agents to trade funds are always crowded with people.

Insiders of the Chinese securities market remark that as Chinese people are more aware of the financial products, especially under the impacts of those products with high profits like stocks and funds, they are more and more likely to invest instead of saving. This has resulted in a profound change in the family property and financial structure. Experts predict that gold is likely to become the next important investment interest following investments in the stock market, bond market, options and futures market, the stamps market, real estate and insurance markets. Additionally, collecting antiques, paintings and other artistic works is considered by some Chinese as a way to manage their money.

走出国门看世界

从20世纪80年代初，泰国、新加坡、马来西亚三国成为第一批在中国实行ADS签证的出境旅游目的地国家开始，出境旅游渐渐成为中国人生活方式的一部分。随后，韩国、尼泊尔、柬埔寨、德国、南非、埃及、澳大利亚、阿根廷等近百个已经执行ADS签证的国家步其后尘，成为中国人的出境游目的地。而签证政策的松紧不光影响中国人的出游，对那些急欲在华揽客

的境外旅游机构同样至关重要。

2002年，欧洲国家德国率先对中国公民开放了旅游签证。不到两年，德国就从中受益多多，在德国过夜的中国游客年增长超过12.5%。而德国仅仅是中国人欧洲游的第一站，英国、法国、瑞士……纷纷放开了对中国的个人旅游签证，希望以此吸引深度旅游的中国人在他们国家作更长时间的停留。

由于美国和加拿大没有成为中国公民出境旅游的目的地国家，中国人赴美、加旅游还存在一定的障碍。但许多驻华机构、商贸公司，甚至大使馆都在尝试各种方式打开这道门！美国大使馆已在北京开始向资质良好的旅行社提供数量有限的团队游客ADS面签，希望能够提升20%的赴美签证率。

到目前，中国出境目的地已多达131个，中国人的出行选择越来越多。而根据多家旅行社的问卷调查，对于许多中国人来说，美国和台湾是他们最想去的旅行目的地。

Seeing the World Abroad

Since Thailand, Singapore and Malaysia became the first tourism destinations granting ADS visas to Chinese in the early 1980s, traveling abroad has gradually become a way of life for the Chinese people. Nearly 100 countries which have practiced

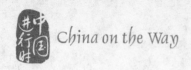

granting ADS visas, including Thailand, Singapore, South Korea, Nepal, Cambodia, Germany, South Africa, Egypt, Australia, and Argentina, have become tourism destinations for Chinese people. Obtaining a visa remains an essential step for the Chinese people hoping to travel abroad, and is of paramount importance to those overseas travel agencies eager to solicit Chinese tourists.

In 2002, Germany was the first European country to grant tourist visas to the Chinese people. In less than two years, Germany has drawn benefit from it, as the numbers of Chinese tourists who spent the night in Germany increased at an annual rate of over 12.5%. However, Germany is only the first stop for Chinese people visiting Europe. Britain, France, Switzerland and other European countries began granting visas to Chinese citizens in the hope of attracting more business from Chinese tourists expecting to stay for a longer period.

Currently, the US and Canada have not yet become tourist destinations for the Chinese people, who thus meet with certain obstacles in visiting these two countries. But a large number of foreign agencies in China, foreign businesses, and even foreign embassies in China are trying every means to improve access to ADS visas. The US Embassy in China has begun to provide ADS visas granted face to face for a limited number of tourist groups intending to travel with reputable Chinese travel agencies, visas granted to Chinese tourists will be increased at 20%.

So far, there are a total of 131 foreign tourist destinations open to the Chinese people, who have more and more opportunity

to travel abroad. The top two destinations for the Chinese people, according to surveys conducted by many travel services, are the US and Taiwan of China.

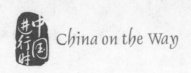
网上购物新时尚

夏天的一个周末,刚刚踏入社会的林小姐有了第一次网上购物的经历。她原本约好同事上街买裙子,可是想到公共汽车拥挤、天气炎热,她就放弃了上街购物的念头。她在家里打开电脑,选择了网上购物。很快,足不出户的她就收到了快递员送来的她订购的裙子和一双漂亮的鞋子……后来她发现自己越来越依赖这种购物方式了,以至于买零食居然也想上网!

"不出门就能买到心仪的商品,网络购物实在太方便了!"林小姐一说起网上购物就眉飞色舞。

如今,随着网络的迅速普及,网上购物已经成为一种时尚的消费方式:节省时间、节约费用、操作方便。你只需坐在家里点点鼠标,登录购物网站,就能看到琳琅满目的货品,门类齐全,从大米、啤酒,到电脑、手机、照相机……敲敲键盘,立刻就可以买到自己喜欢的商品。这种新鲜、便捷的购物方式深受众多网民尤其是年轻人的青睐。

　　"网络购物也不只是年轻人的专利。"步入中年的杨女士坦言。今年情人节,在外地出差的老公就通过网上购物的方式送给她一串珍珠项链。收到项链的一刹那,她在惊喜之余,不禁感叹信息时代带给人们的全新感受。

　　相关调查结果显示,如今"网购"越来越红火,其原因不外乎两点:一是因为大大节省了租赁铺面的成本,所以网络店铺货品价格比实体店铺肯定便宜很多,可以吸引很多买家;二是网络店铺可以24小时营业,并且向全世界买家开放,这也是传统店铺所无法做到的。

　　网上购物虽然轻松、便捷,却也有诸多不利,一不留神或许就碰上个骗局。深圳的王先生在一个名为《益民购物网》的网站上发现有大量手机销售信息,而且售价均比市价低三成左右。于是他就按要求通过银行汇去了

1100多元购机款，对方称将通过邮政EMS特快专递将货发给他。可是隔日，网站又通知他往指定账号存入3000元风险保证金才可交货。王先生这时意识到陷入了骗局，于是断然拒绝对方要求，并要求退款，可对方不再接听他的电话，而且他使用过的电脑再也无法登陆该网站，因对方设置了禁止王先生的IP地址访问。王先生为贪便宜上当受骗，后悔莫及。王先生的教训也提醒了广大消费者：网上购物是方便，可千万得"悠着点"。

Shopping Online — A New Fashion

During a recent summer weekend, Miss Lin, who had just graduated from school not long before, did her first online shopping. Actually, she had asked her colleague to shop with her at a mall for a skirt, but the thought of the crowded buses and hot weather made her change her mind. She chose instead to turn on the computer and shop at home online. Without being bothered to go out, she got a skirt and a pair of beautiful shoes. As time passed, she found herself more and more addicted to this way of shopping, so much so that she even bought her snacks online!

"You can have the stuff you want delivered to your front door without going out for shopping. How convenient online shopping is!" said Miss Lin excitedly.

Nowadays, as computers and the Internet become rapidly more accessible, online shopping has become a fashionable way to consume. It saves time and money and is easy to do. With a click of the mouse you may log in to the online stores where an amazing variety of commodities are available, ranging from rice and beer to computers, cell phones and cameras. Since people can buy whatever they like by simply clicking the mouse, online shopping is very popular, particularly among the young netizens.

"Shopping online is not only favored by young people," the middle-aged Ms. Yang remarked frankly. Though her husband was out of town for business on Valentine's Day, he bought her a pearl necklace as a gift through a website. The moment she received the gift, exhilarated she was, she could not help marveling at this new experience brought about by the information era.

Some related surveys indicate that at present, there are two primary reasons for the increasing popularity of online shopping: First, in the virtual cyber world, one does not need to rent a building or storefront to run business, thus saving a considerable amount of money in overhead, leading to lower prices for most commodities. Second, online shops may be available around the clock to the whole world, which is beyond the capability of the traditional storefront.

Simple and convenient as online shopping is, there are still hazards such as cheats and traps which you may run into unconsciously. Mr. Wang from Shenzhen discovered a website called Yimin Shopping Net offering cell phones with prices thirty percent lower than the average market prices. He wired 1,100 yuan

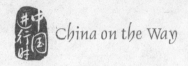

to the bank account as required for his purchase and was told that the cell phone would be delivered by EMS. However, the next day, Mr. Wang was requested by the website to deposit another 3000 yuan into the given bank account as a security deposit before the cell phone would be sent to him. It was at this moment that Mr. Wang realized this was a trap. He firmly refused the payment and asked for a refund. No one answered his calls and his computer's IP address was blocked from the website. Initially believing he had found a best buy, Mr. Wang regretfully had to pay for his greed. His lesson serves as a reminder for all consumers: When you enjoy the convenience of online shopping, be ever vigilant against fraud.

新年俗：手机短信拜年忙

随着现代通讯手段的发展，中国人的拜年方式从上门拜访逐渐演变为多种形式，如寄明信片、打电话、发网络贺卡等等，尤其是短信拜年的方式最为盛行，它已成为中国人的新年俗。

2007年农历猪年春节，

一些手机短信祝词分外流行:

"人逢盛世情无限,猪拱华门岁有余。人增福寿年增岁,鱼满池塘猪满栏。"

"愿你抱着平安,拥着健康,揣着幸福,携着快乐,搂着温馨,带着甜蜜,牵着财运,拽着吉祥,迈入猪年,快乐度过每一天!"

许多这样的猪年春节短信在亲朋好友间大量转发传递。信息时代的传统春节,因这些飞来飞去的手机祝福短信,变得格外有滋味。

据统计,猪年春节的七天长假期间,中国手机短信的发送总量约140亿条,精彩纷呈的拜年短信在中国4.7亿手机用户间穿梭如流。随着手机普及率的提高,越来越多的中国人习惯于发短信交换信息和传递情感。据统计,从2000年的发送总量仅10亿余条,到目前的3000亿条,七年间,中国手机短信发送量增长了约300倍。

短信能如此深入中国人的生活,不仅因其实惠,还由于现代人工作生活高速运转,活动半径扩大,频率加快,传统交流方式难以适应,人们自然会选择高效便捷的手机短信;更深层次的原因则在于,以简短文字来传递信息、传达情感,更符合东方人含蓄、婉转的表达习惯。

New Year, New Custom — Greetings by Short Messages through Cell Phones

With the development of modern communication technologies, Chinese traditional ways of greeting each other in Spring Festival have gradually taken many forms such as sending postcards, making phone calls, sending electronic greeting cards on the Internet. One method in particular, greeting by cellular phone text messages, is the most popular way and has become a new custom in greeting Spring Festival for the Chinese.

2007 is the year of pig in the lunar calendar, contributing to the amazing popularity of short messages related to pigs. Here are some examples:

"We live in a prosperous era - much gratitude to express; Pig pushes open the door to wealth - great fortunes to wish for."

"People become a year older as New Year comes, with ponds abounding with fish and pigpens full of pigs- another affluent year is coming."

"May you be surrounded by peace, health, happiness, joys, warmth, sweetness, large fortunes, and good luck in the year of pig! Happy every day!"

These short messages are sent and distributed in large number among friends and relatives, adding special fun to the traditional

festivals in the information era.

According to the statistics, during the seven-day-holiday of Spring Festival, the total number of text messages sent by cell phones reached around 14 billion. Novel and interesting short messages of all kinds have spread among the 470 million cell phone users in China. With the increasing popularity of cell phones in China, more and more Chinese are using short messages to exchange information and express their emotions. During the seven years since 2000, the total number of text messages has increased by 300 times from one billion in 2000 to 300 billion this year.

The reasons why text messages have impacted Chinese people so much are more than one. The first is due to their low cost. Moreover, in a fast-paced modern society traditional ways of communication have become out of date. Naturally, people would like to turn to a more efficient and convenient way. Perhaps most significantly, the short format of text messaging is ideally suited for cultures such as those of the East whose people traditionally convey information and express emotions in a reserved and implicit manner.

享受休闲

　　许多年前，"休闲"一词很少被中国人提及，人们更难有时间去享受它。1995年中国开始实行了双休日制度；1999年又实行"五一、十一、春节黄金周"。自此，中国人才有了充分的时间享受长假带来

的快乐，"休闲"才真正步入他们的生活。

休闲时光如何度过？据一项调查显示，46.46%的人选择了旅游。2006年中国的旅游人数达13.94亿人次，出境旅游的总人数达3000多万人次。出境游的目的地已从新、马、泰扩展到欧洲、非洲的21个国家和地区。

其次是运动、健身。据北京零点调查公司对北京、上海、广州等五个城市的消费调查发现，北京平均每人每年用于体育健身的消费达到888元，在五个城市中名列第一。每当周末或假日，一些体育馆、球场内便人头攒动。运动、健身不仅可带给人们快乐，也帮助人们缓解压力、健康体魄，使身心放松。

休闲时光里，还有越来越多的人选择学习充电。国家图书馆每逢节假日都坐满了大量阅读者。据悉，国家图书馆每天要接待借阅者1万多人。人们也舍得花钱、花时间学习多种技能，获得考级证书。考研培训、新东方英语培训、雅思英语培训、MBA研修班、通讯软件人才培训、金融分析师考前辅导等一批新兴培训应运而生，分外红火。

艺术欣赏、插花、茶艺、收藏等丰富多彩的休闲方式，在人们的生活中日渐时兴。每逢周末或假日，那些大大小小的茶艺馆、酒吧、咖啡屋、网吧，就成了人们休闲的港湾，也构成了城市的一道道浪漫风景线。

多元的休闲方式反映了中国人在满足物质生活需求的同时，开始讲求生活品位，注重精神方面的消费，追求舒畅、惬意的生活。

Enjoy Leisure

Many years ago, almost no one in China took an interest in the word "leisure", let alone afforded the time to enjoy the concept. In 1995, China began practicing the system of the two-day weekend holiday. In 1999, it incorporated "golden-week holidays" on May Day, National Day and Spring Festival. Since then, Chinese people have had more time to enjoy the pleasure of long holidays, and "leisure" has genuinely stepped into their lives.

How are leisure hours spent? According to a recent survey, 46.46% of Chinese people choose traveling. In 2006 domestic tourists and international tourists totaled 1.394 billion and over 30 million respectively. Tourist destinations abroad ranged from Singapore, Malaysia and Thailand to 21 countries or regions in Europe, Africa and other continents.

Sports and body building have also gradually become popular activities for Chinese people. Beijing Horizon Research Consultancy Group conducted a survey on consumption in Beijing, Shanghai, Guangzhou and other two cities, finding that in Beijing the *per capita* expenses for sports and body building add up to 888 yuan each year, ranking first of the five cities. On weekends or holidays,

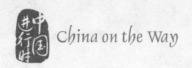

gymnasiums and fitness clubs are crowded with people, enjoying the pleasure of various sports and body building exercises, and relaxing body and soul.

Additionally, leisure hours are increasingly being used by many people to pursue further studies. The National Library of China during festivals or holidays is said to receive 10,000-odd book borrowers every day. People spend money and time in learning new skills and earning graded examination certificates. Training for graduate school entrance examination, English training, IELTS training, MBA programs, IT skills training, pre-examination tutoring for financial analysts and other emerging trainings are booming.

Personal hobbies such as art appreciation, flower arrangement, the art of tea, antique collection, and other varied and colorful means of cultural leisure are on the upswing in people's life. On weekends or holidays, teahouses, pubs, coffeehouses and cyber bars have become hot places in cities.

The pluralistic means of leisure show that Chinese people cater to the material needs in their life, meanwhile start to pursue more satisfaction by seeking a higher quality life with less mental stress.

中国农民还离不开炕

　　和成千上万的中国东北人一样，73岁的李秀兰在炕上作息。炕是由砖块砌成用来睡觉的平台，在漫长的寒冬季节能用煤炭和稻草烧热取暖。

　　千百年来，炕一直是中国北方地区居民起居的重要场所。一家人挤在炕上，吃饭、睡觉。在炕上，孩子们能玩闹着度过一整天。"我们这里靠近西伯利

亚，下午三时天就黑了，温度能低到零下40摄氏度。如果没什么事，我们整天都待在炕上。"住在靠近中俄边境的桦川地区的27岁的农民周玉红说。

在北方一些中小城市里人们已基本不用煤取暖了，暖气成为主要的取暖方式。但在农村，尽管有手机、互联网等现代科技的冲击，炕在很多地方还是被保留了下来。因为对很多家庭来说，炕才是最完美的选择：烧炕用的秸秆不用花钱，炕保温的时间比较长。在寒冷的冬日，一家人聚在炕上看电视、聊天，甚至喝茶娱乐，其乐融融。"天气变冷了，每个人都必须有个炕，"周玉红的公公说，"没有炕，你过不了冬。"

据估计，在中国的东北地区，大概有80%—90%的农户还在使用炕。短期内，炕不会消失，因为当地农民非常依赖它。

Kang, Still Loved by Northern Farmers

Like thousands of Chinese living in the northeast, 73-year-old Li Xiulan still maintains the habit of working and sleeping on

her *kang*, a brick bed heated by coal and straw against the piercing cold and commonly found in northern China.

For centuries, *kang* has remained the center of everyday life in northern China. In winter, the whole family will huddle on it, having dinners or going to sleep. The children may play the whole day on the warm brick bed. "Here is close to Siberia. It gets dark at three in the afternoon, and the temperature can drop to 40 degrees below zero. We usually stay on the *kang* all day," says Zhou Yuhong, a 27-year-old farmer living in Huachuan near the border area between China and Russia.

Nowadays, more modern heating devices have replaced coal for keeping warm in small and medium-sized northern cities, leaving no space for the traditional *kang*. But in rural areas brick beds are still kept in many places, even though cell phones and the Internet have changed much the way of living. For many families, *kang* is the best choice. Straw can be found anywhere, costs nothing and keeps the *kang* warm for quite a long time. On cold winter days, the whole family stay on their *kang*, watching TV, chatting and drinking tea, cosy and happy. "It's getting cold. Everybody must have his *kang*," says Zhou Yuhong's father-in-law. "Otherwise, you can't make do in the cold winter."

It's said that *kang* is still popular in 80-90% of the farming households in the northeast. *Kang* will remain as long as the farmers love it.

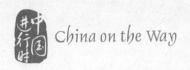
中国人热衷寻家谱

现在，中国的"家谱追寻热"逐渐升温。"我是唐太宗李世民的子孙"、"我是成吉思汗的后代"，对家谱津津乐道的中国人明显增多。"证明明代文人某某子孙的家谱被发现，唐代某位皇帝的子孙现生活在某某地方"的报道也不时见诸报端。在古城西安，甚至还出现了以代人寻找祖先及家谱为业的人。

中国人追寻家谱的热情源自对"家"执著的依恋。每年春节，数以亿计的中国人想方设法从四面八方赶回家过年。这样的情形使人对中国人的家族观念感叹不已。家族文化是中国传统文化的一个根基，家谱的保存和延续是家族文化的一种体现。而在新中国建立后的一段时期，中国人的这种观念曾被迫趋于淡漠。首先是20世纪50年代中国农村实行的人民公社制度，它在许多方面改变了人们根深蒂固的传统家族关系。1958年的大跃进时代还实行了一段吃"大锅饭"的试验，这种与家庭以外的陌生人同吃

同住的形式
不久即宣告
失败。

　　除人民
公社外，中
国各地的
"单位生活"
也取代了中
国的家族制。
比如说，《人
民日报》社
的员工及其
家庭成员都
在《人民日
报》这个单

位中生活。单位提供包括员工工作、住房甚至包括他
们子女上学的学校、医院等所有满足生活所需的设
施。单位一时间成为中国人的"家"。

　　20多年前的改革开放以后，人民公社取消了，人
们头脑中的计划经济理念和单位观念也发生了很大
变化。特别是近年来中国传统文化的复苏和不断升
温，人们开始重新关注家族血统关系，伴随而来的就
是在中国人中兴起了一股寻根热潮。在北京最大的
书店西单图书大厦里，揭示姓氏起源的书籍始终畅

销不衰。而在有些著名的旅游胜地，还有兜售写有"某某氏之源"、解释姓氏的说明书。

在浙江、广东，寻根问祖、修建供奉祖先灵位的祠堂已成为一些先富起来的人们的流行时尚。在有中国"顶级富豪之乡"之称的温州和义乌等地，大部分人都以家庭手工业作坊，即家庭式作业起家。他们从手工作坊开始，逐步发展成为家族型中小企业。曾出版过《中国家族企业研究》一书的作者甘德安先生认为，改革开放以后，中国内部发展起来的企业90%是家族企业。

中国人的世界观起源于家族。关系亲近就可以相互称兄道弟。再者，如果大家利益、意见一致，即使你是韩国人或者美国人，他们也可以毫不犹豫地称你为一家人。这种家族意识带动了以家庭为单位的家庭经济的发展，活跃了市场，对中国经济发展起了积极的推动作用。但是，从另一个角度来看，中国人的"家"也是封建社会中社会构成的核心要素。它也可能产生腐败与家庭利己主义，甚至还会引起那些由血缘及类似观念结成的集团间的矛盾纠纷。这也正是中国学者所担心的一个重要问题。不知这种家族观念的复苏对中国社会是幸还是不幸。

Tracing Family Tree

In China there is a growing interest in genealogy with more Chinese eager to discover their family heritage. Some people are heard saying that "I am the descendent of Taizong Emperor Li Shimin of the Tang Dynasty" or "Genghis Khan is my ancestor". In Xi'an, an ancient capital, there are even people tracing back ancestors or family trees as their profession.

The enthusiasm for tracing family tree originates from a persistent love of family by the Chinese. Every Spring Festival, driven by a strong sense of home attachment, hundreds of millions of Chinese from all corners of the country will try their best to return to their hometown for a reunion. Books on the origins of family names remain best sellers for many seasons regardless whether they are found in the biggest bookstore in the bustling shopping district of Xidan in Beijing, or in the famous tourist destination of the Ming Tombs.

In Wenzhou and Yiwu, places regarded as the land of great fortune, many family-run businesses are booming. Rich residents in these areas, as in Guangdong Province, consider it a trendy thing to trace back their roots and build shrines for their ancestral tablets.

The world view of the Chinese originates from the family and clan. Chinese regard people with whom they have a close relationship as brothers or family members, no matter what their nationality. A strong sense of family and clan lays the foundation

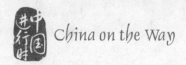 China on the Way

for the growth of the family economy with family as the basic unit, and family economy is an active part of the market and contributes to the growth of the country. Yet, of concern to some Chinese scholars, the sense of family and clan could result in corruption, egoism, or even conflicts between different blood groups or groups clustered out of family mentality.

第二篇
文化与符号
CULTURE & SYMBOL

红红火火"中国红"

精美纷呈"中国结"

旗袍，恒久的东方魅力

"福"字倒，福运到

中国人爱喝茶

姚明——中国人的骄傲

红红火火"中国红"

中国著名导演张艺谋在其执导的《大红灯笼高高挂》和《英雄》等影片中，巧妙地运用了红灯笼、红衣、红绸等充满中国风情的红色，渲染了浓重的中国艺术气息和格调，给观众以强烈的东方美感和视觉享受。

红色在中国代表着兴旺发达、红红火火、大吉大利。在中国人心目中，红色是喜庆、吉祥的颜色，亦有热烈、温暖、热闹、浪漫、祈福、辟邪的丰富含义。"见红大吉"早已成了中华民族的传统文化心理。从古至今，红色点缀着中国人的生活和节庆。

对红色的崇尚，最早可追溯到远古时代的人们对日神、火神的崇拜。旧石器时代的山顶洞人就用红色染绘饰物。到了汉朝，汉高祖刘邦自称"赤帝之子"，此后红色广泛流行，成了庶民百姓们崇尚的颜色。汉朝以后，中国人尚红的风俗就一直沿袭下来，直至今天。中国红已深深植根于中华民族的传统和风尚之中。

从朱门红墙到红木箱柜；从孩子的贴身红肚兜到本命年的红腰带；从添丁进口时门楣上挂的红布条，到老寿星的红寿服和红寿桃；从深闺女儿的红头绳，到扭秧歌时的红舞绸；从开张大吉的剪红彩，到恭贺新禧的红贺卡；从象征权力的红印泥，到记录功勋的红锦旗；从闻名遐迩的唐三彩，到景德镇的"祭

红"瓷……中国红无时不在，无处不在。

中国红在爱情与婚庆中不可或缺。相思有红豆，定情有红绣球，彩礼称为"花红"。新婚洞房满目红艳：红门帘、红窗帘、红被子、红床单、红枕头、红双喜、红蜡烛；新娘坐红轿、穿红裙、盖红盖头，新郎骑红马、扎红花。所有这些都为婚礼增添了热烈而喜庆的气氛。

中国红在年节时表现得更为生动。迎新春时，家家户户要挂红灯、贴红对联、剪红窗花，连孩子们放的鞭炮、得的压岁钱，也皆是红纸包装，称为红炮、红包。听听这首民谣："新年到，新年到，老人着新衣，小孩戴红帽，满街红红绿绿，好热闹。"

蕴涵着丰厚的东方风情的"中国红"展现了中华民族积极向上的精神气质，它是中国人喜爱的色彩。

The Flourishing "Chinese Red"

In such movies as *Red Lanterns* and *Hero*, China's famous director Zhang Yimou cleverly used red lanterns, red costumes, red silk and other red symbols, creating a strong atmosphere of Chinese art, a striking sense of oriental beauty, and intense visual pleasure.

In China, the color red signifies prosperity, growing afflu-ence and good fortune. In the eyes of the Chinese people, red is a

joyful and auspicious color, transmitting such meanings as fervor, warmth, bustling activity, romance, aspiration for happiness, and exorcism. "Good luck at the sight of red" has always been a sort of cultural psychology according to Chinese tradition. From time immemorial, red has decorated Chinese people's lives and their festive ceremonies.

The advocacy of red traces back to ancient times, when people worshipped the god of sun and the god of fire. During the Stone Age, the Upper Cave Man dyed their ornaments with red coloring. Emperor Liu Bang of the Han Dynasty claimed to be the "Son of the Red Emperor". Since then, red has become widely popular with Chinese people and has lasted to this day. Chinese red is rooted in Chinese tradition.

Examples of traditions involving the color red are manifold, from including a red door or wall in the home or business to placement of a red wooden box as a decoration. An infant is traditionally protected by the placement of a red undergarment over his or her abdomen, and a red belt fastened around a person's waist is worn for luck during the recurrent year of the animal when one was born. Births are celebrated with a red strip of cloth hung down the lintel of a Chinese house and the elderly wear red garments in celebration of their birthday as they share red birthday peaches. As personal adornment a red string may be used for binding a girl's plaits or a piece of red silk may be worn in a *yangge* dance. The auspicious beginning of a business is heralded by the cutting of a red ribbon and wishes for a prosperous new year are shared with red greeting cards. From a red ink paste used to affix a seal to symbolize

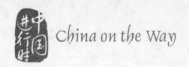

a person's power to a red silk banner recording a person's meritorious deeds, from the well-known tricolor glazed pottery of the Tang Dynasty to the bright red porcelain manufactured in Jingdezhen… Chinese red is ubiquitous at any time.

Chinese red is indispensable in love and wedding ceremonies. Red beans are a token of love; a girl tosses a red silk ball to a man as a pledge of her love for him; betrothal gifts are called "Hua Hong" (flower red); a nuptial chamber is imbued with red: red door or window curtains, red quilts, red bed sheets, red pillows, red Chinese characters "Shuang Xi (double happiness)", and red candles; a bride sitting in a sedan chair wears a red skirt and a red bridal veil covering her head during the wedding ceremony, and a bridegroom wears a large red flower as he approaches on his horse. All these add a lively and joyful atmosphere to the wedding ceremony.

Chinese red is embodied more vividly during Spring Festival, when all households will hang red lanterns, paste red antithetical couplets, and cut red paper for window decorations, and children will light red firecrackers and receive the lunar New Year gift money wrapped in red paper. According to a folk rhyme, "When the lunar New Year is drawing near, the old wear new clothes and the young have on red hats; the bustling streets are filled with red and green."

Teeming with profound philosophical tradition, Chinese red, a color loved by Chinese people, shows their love of life as they forge ahead energetically.

精美纷呈"中国结"

每逢中国年节，无论你走在中国的城市商业街，还是世界各地的唐人街，那些琳琅满目、形态各异、美丽飘逸的"中国结"都会出现在你的眼前，让你感受到浓浓的中国韵味扑面而来。

"中国结"全称为"中国传统装饰结"。它有悠久的历史，是渗透中华民族

特有的文化底蕴的一种手工编织工艺品。"结"与"吉"谐音，蕴含"幸福吉祥、长寿安康、财物丰盛、团圆美满、喜庆欢乐"等祈福的意义，它作为民间祝祷的符号，一直流传至今。

中国结不仅形态美，还因其不同用途各有不同

含义的得名，如婚礼时新房装饰的中国结叫做"盘长结"，寓意一对新人相随相依，永不分离；在佩玉上装饰的叫"如意结"，寓含称心如意，万事如意；扇子上装饰的"吉祥结"，代表大吉大利，祥瑞美好；烟袋上装饰"蝴蝶结"，"蝴"与"福"谐音，表示福到眼前；本命年腰系"红绳结"，祈求驱病除灾，一年安顺；汽车前挂"顺风结"，寓意"一路顺风"，"一路平安"。这些"结"早已超出了实用功能，成为富有美感和寓意的吉祥饰物。

今天，中国结在不断传承、发掘和市场开发中，变得愈发丰富多彩，精美纷呈，成了许多人心目中富有东方文化神韵的中国符号。

Chinese Knot:
Delicate in Varied Splendor

During Spring Festival, a great variety of beautiful and graceful Chinese knots on the commercial streets of Chinese cities or in the Chinatowns throughout the world bring a strong Chinese flavor.

The full name of a "Chinese knot" is a "traditional Chinese decorative knot". Having a long history, the knot handicraft is infiltrated with a cultural meaning unique for Chinese people. The homophonic Chinese characters "Jie (knot)" and "Ji (auspicious)" imply people's praying for "happiness and

auspiciousness", "longevity and healthiness", "abundant property", "family reunion and satisfaction", and "jubilation and happiness". A symbol used to pray for good fortune, the Chinese knot has been passed down to this day.

A beautifully-shaped Chinese knot boasts of different names containing various meanings owing to many kinds of uses. For example, the Chinese knot used to decorate the nuptial chamber at the wedding ceremony is called "Pan (coiling around) Chang (long) Jie (knot)", indicating that the new couple will keep each other company and never part from each other. The Chinese knot ornamented on a jade pendant is named "Ruyi (complete satisfaction) Jie (knot)", referring to complete satisfaction or success in everything. The "Jixiang (auspiciousness) Jie (knot)" adorning a fan represents auspiciousness or good fortune. The "Hudie Jie (bowtie)" ornamenting a tobacco pipe implies the advent of "Fu" (happiness), as "Hu" and "Fu" are homophonic Chinese characters. The "Hong (red) Sheng (rope) Jie (knot)" fastened around a person's waist in the recurrent year of the animal when one was born suggests the elimination of diseases or disasters, as well as security and success all the year round. The "Shun (favorable) Feng (wind) Jie (knot)" hung in the front of a car signifies a pleasant journey or a nice trip. Today, these knots have exceeded their practical use and have become mascots containing a sense of beauty and rich connotations.

Today, the traditional Chinese knot is carried forward, and may be found in various shops. It has become a colorful and delicate Chinese symbol offering a flavor of oriental culture.

旗袍，恒久的东方魅力

从嘎纳电影节上身着红色旗袍礼服的国际影星巩俐，到电影《花样年华》中身着精致传统旗袍的张曼玉，美人佳衣，演绎出东方万种风情。

旗袍是中华女性传统服装的典型代表，中华服饰文化的精华。旗袍的整体造型和风韵，充分表现出东方女子贤淑、典雅、温柔、清丽的性情与气质，其魅力和文化内涵使之在中国民族服装中独领风骚，久盛而不衰。

"旗袍"源自古代蒙古游牧民族的袍服，后来演变为清代满族女子服装，称"旗袍"。20

世纪20年代，旗袍经过改良在上海妇女中流行开来。这种旗袍吸纳了西式剪裁方法，加入了连衣裙、晚礼服等时装的元素，显得幽雅而时尚。当年，孙中山夫人宋庆龄身穿新式改良的绸缎旗袍出现在汉口的国民政府阅兵观礼台上，她的倡导使新式旗袍很快风靡了中国的大江南北。此后的三四十年代，旗袍一直随着流行时尚变革出新，它不仅是中国妇女的日常服装，更成为上流社会女子的时髦装扮。后至六七十年代，受"文革"影响，旗袍一度销声匿迹，中国内地很少有人穿了。

近年来，各种各样的新式旗袍又重新在中国的城市里流行起来，在一些庆典、喜宴、迎宾场合，不少妇女喜欢穿旗袍和传统服装，以示隆重和表现东方女子的风韵。新式旗袍在结构上仍保留了女性胸、腰、臀三围突出的优美曲线，在色彩、剪裁、搭配上也融入了现代时装元素和时代气息。

旗袍还是外交场合代表中国妇女形象的礼服，其款式和花样绚丽高贵。礼服旗袍不仅由丝绸、锦缎、平绒等面料精工制作，还加入了刺绣、挑花、绘画等传统艺术的装饰手段，显得高贵而典雅。

在一些国际时装展会上，东方旗袍常常成为设计师灵感的源泉之一。法国的服装大师皮尔·卡丹就曾说自己从中国旗袍中获取了大量灵感。2004年，在为伊夫圣罗兰的天才设计师汤姆·福特举办的告别YSL

的时装秀上，一系列中国式的长衫旗袍与欧式长靴的搭配，让人领略了来自东方的时尚风采。

美丽的中国旗袍，还会随时代不断变化，并以其独具的魅力融入世界服装文化之苑。旗袍的魅力永存！

Cheongsam: Everlasting Oriental Charm

From international movie star Gong Li, wearing a red cheongsam at the Cannes Film Festival, to Maggie Cheung who was dressed in several delicate traditional cheongsams in the film *In the Mood for Love*, beautifully dressed Chinese women of graceful bearing have provided audiences worldwide with a visual feast.

Cheongsam, a close-fitting dress with a high neck and a slit skirt as worn by women in the Manchu ethnic group, is a style of traditional Chinese costume representing the cream of the Chinese fashion culture. Its shape and charm completely embody oriental women's virtuous, elegant, gentle, and graceful temperament, and

its glamour and cultural connotations make it ever popular as it plays a leading role in China's national fashion style.

Cheongsams date back to ancient times, originating from the robes worn by the nomadic Mongolian ethnic group. These later evolved into the garments worn by women of the Manchu ethnic group of the Qing Dynasty, called "*chi-pao*." In the 1920s, cheongsams were improved and became popular with women in Shanghai. Incorporating a Western style tailoring method and the elements of one-piece dresses and evening dresses, they looked elegant and fashionable. Once, Sun Yat-sen's wife Soong Ching Ling wearing a newly improved silk cheongsam was present at the National Government's stand for reviewing a military parade in Hankou. Her advocacy made the new-style cheongsam nationally popular overnight. In the 1930s and 1940s, cheongsams in new styles were constantly brought forth in the most current fashions of the time. These were not only garments for daily wear, but also fashionable dresses worn by upper-class women in Shanghai. During the Cultural Revolution, cheongsams disappeared from fashion on the Chinese mainland.

In the past few years, various new-style cheongsams have become popular again in cities. At certain celebrations and wedding banquets or on reception occasions, many women enjoy wearing cheongsams and other traditional Chinese garments to incarnate the solemnity of the ceremonies and the charm of oriental women. The new-style cheongsams retain the graceful curves formed by a woman's body and incorporate elements of modern fashions and the spirit of the times in terms of color,

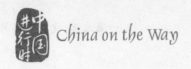

tailoring and arrangement.

Also, cheongsams, with their gorgeous and splendid styles and designs, often serve as the preferred style of dress for women representing China on diplomatic occasions. Dress cheongsams, exquisitely made out of silk, satin, velveteen and other materials and blended with such traditional means of decoration as embroidery and painting, appear noble and elegant.

Cheongsams are coming into vogue at international fashion shows as well. In particular, some cheongsams, decorated with images of birds, flowers, and even images of Beijing Opera style makeup and designed in an original and exaggerative manner, vividly reveal the glamour of Chinese garments and their cultural charm, winning good graces.

Fashion designers often draw inspiration from classical costumes such as cheongsam. French fashion designer Pierre Cardin once admitted that he had gotten much inspiration from Chinese cheongsams. In 2004, at the fashion show held in honor of Tom Ford, a talented fashion designer from Yves Saint Laurent (YSL), a series of Chinese gowns and cheongsams matched with European-style high boots brought the charm of Eastern fashions to the audience.

The beautiful Chinese cheongsam will constantly change with the times, and will, by virtue of its unique and everlasting charm, forever be an important contributor to world fashion culture.

"福"字倒，福运到

　　每逢新春佳节，中国的家家户户都要在屋门、窗叶、墙壁、门楣、箱柜上贴大大小小的"福"字，迎春接福。张贴"福"字早已成为中国人的传统习俗。

　　"福"字，一般解释为"幸福"，在中国人的心目中则指"福气、福运"。春节贴"福"字，无论现在还是过去，都寄托了人们对幸福生活的向往，对美好未来的祝愿。

　　贴"福"字在民间很有讲究，常把"福"字倒过来贴，"倒"与"到"同音，表示"福气、福运"会来到。

过去，"福"字常要请乡里文人用笔墨书写，而现在市场、商店里出售的均是将"福"字和一些吉祥图案，如寿星、寿桃、鲤鱼跳龙门、五谷丰登、龙凤呈祥等一起精描细绘成的吉祥画，人们可随意挑选，装扮自己的家。

The Chinese Character "Fu" Pasted Upside Down Implies the Advent of Good Fortune

With the advent of Spring Festival, all households in China will paste up large or small Chinese character "Fu" (happiness) on their doors, windows, walls, lintels, and box frames. It has become a traditional practice for the Chinese people to put up the Chinese character "Fu" for the purpose of greeting the arrival of spring and praying for happiness.

The Chinese character "Fu", generally interpreted as "happiness", means "good luck" or "good fortune" in the minds of the Chinese people. "Fu" posted during Spring Festival has always signified people's yearning for a happy life, as well as a wish for a

brilliant future.

It is quite an art to put up "Fu", which should be pasted up-side down. The homonymous Chinese characters "Dao (upside down)" and "Dao (arrival)" allude to the advent of "Fu (good fortune)."

In addition, many Chinese people paint various auspicious pictures incorporating "Fu", along with such propitious designs as the god of longevity, the birthday peach, the carp leaping into the dragon's gate (gaining fame and advancement), the abundant harvest of all food crops, and the prosperity brought by the dragon and the phoenix (extremely good fortune). The pictures pasted on front doors take on an auspicious, joyful and beautiful look during holidays. The Chinese character "Fu" was once written by rural calligraphers, but now in the markets or at shops is sold all sorts of red paper printed with "Fu", as well as various auspicious pictures with different designs.

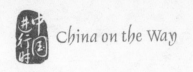

中国人爱用模糊词

当问及中国人对某事或某人的看法时，得到的回答通常是"还行、凑合、差不多"。更糟糕的情况，就用"不太好"。除非你不停地追问，他们很少使用"好、坏"这样绝对的说法，这让外国人很难揣测到中国人内心真实的想法。

韩国人与中国人做生意时，听到中国人说"好"，便想当然地认为谈判非常顺利。但随着谈判的进行，他们发现结果大相径庭，这令韩国人很生气，认为明明已经说好的事情，怎么又变了呢？

一位在北京生活、经商近十年的韩国人认为，千万不要以为中国人说"好"，就一切万事大吉了。中国人的意思仅仅是"是的，您的意思我明白了"。

中国人认为，世上的事情瞬息万变，立即作决定非常困难；同时，中国人也非常重视整体效果，他们通常是在仔细观察了周围的情况后，才回答对错、好坏。生意与日常生活一样，只有在对整体情况作出判

断后，他们才小心翼翼地提出自己的看法。"见机行事"这样的词语反映出的思维方式已深深融入中国人的意识之中。

中国语言中的模糊性，有其深厚的哲学基础。中国人强调不偏不倚的"中庸之道"。遗憾的是，很多时候，他们对中庸的思考更多地倾向于现实的需要。

Puzzling Fuzzy Words

When asked to comment on someone or something, the Chinese often give a fuzzy answer such as "Ok", "just so-so" or "not bad". Even if the subject really is bad, the answer will be no other than "not good". Unless you keep asking, no one will give a definite "good" or "bad", often puzzling foreigners.

When doing business with the Chinese, the Koreans may believe that their talks will go on smoothly if the Chinese say "good". But later, if the Chinese side changes their attitude or tone, the Koreans will be annoyed: Didn't you agree the other day? Why the sudden change?

A Korean businessman who has stayed in Beijing for nearly 10 years finally cracked the nut: Never take it for granted that everything is fine if the Chinese say "good". Their "good" only means "I see" or "Well, what next then?"

To the Chinese, things are constantly changing, making it

difficult to make a prompt decision. As they value the overall effects, they won't give a "right" or "wrong", a "good" or "bad" until they've made a careful study of the whole situation. It's the same in doing business and in everyday life. They'll squeeze out their judgment only after balancing the advantages and the disadvantages. The phrases of "play it by ear" and "regulate the appetite according to the dishes" are a good reflection of this deep-rooted Chinese way of thinking.

The fuzzy character of the Chinese language has its profound philosophic basis. The Chinese always try to follow the "golden mean", but in many cases, their neutral approach is a compromise to the reality.

中国节有滋味，洋节也红火

　　随着全球化浪潮的涌动，来中国工作、定居的外国人日益增多，中国的节日色彩也日趋多样化。传统节日仍过得有滋有味，西方洋节也给中国人的生活增添了几分色彩。

　　中国的传统节日颇为不少，如春节、元宵节、端午节、中秋节、重阳节等等，还有许多少数民族的民俗节日。对于这些中华民族千百年来逐渐形成的本土节日，近年来，随着传统文化的复兴和发扬光大，人们愈发珍视。更多的商家对传统节日市场进行了新包装、新开发，让节日商品愈发丰富多彩，最

大限度地
满足人们
多样的需
求。普通
百姓则把
这些传统
节日当做
亲人相聚、

合家团圆的最佳日子。春节的年糕、元宵节的汤圆、端午的粽子、中秋的月饼，也成了人们传递亲情、友情的节令佳品。中国人正在把自己的传统节日过得更有滋味。

　　而洋节，例如圣诞节、情人节、感恩节、愚人节、万圣节等等这些外来的节日，同样在中国大行其道，特别受到年轻人的喜爱和追捧。每到洋节来临，各大商场里五花八门的节日礼品格外吸引眼球，年轻人三五成群、邀朋呼友外出娱乐。在2006年圣诞平安夜里，北京成了不夜城。千名中外嘉宾在国宾酒店大宴会厅内共享圣诞晚宴。北京音乐厅还举行了圣诞民族交响音乐会。在后海的酒吧里，许多年轻人饮酒、歌舞、尽情狂欢，格外惬意！

　　有人说，中国有那么多节日，何必还来过洋节呢？其实，除了中国的传统节日外，引进一些外来的节日文化，既能让百姓感受异域文化的风采，又能丰富生活，带来欢乐，增进交流与友情，从商家来说，还能扩大消费，拉动内需，何乐而不为呢？

Foreign Festivals—
No Less Popular than Native Ones

As there are more and more foreigners flooding to work or settle in China under the motivation of globalization, Chinese festivals are becoming more and more diversified. By contrast to the traditional Chinese festivals which are celebrated in various ways, Western festivals have enriched our lives.

China has many traditional festivals such as Spring Festival, Lantern Festival, Dragon Boat Festival, Mid-autumn Day, the Double Ninth Festival, etc. along with some particular festivals celebrated by ethnic minorities. As time passed, these gradually developed into traditional festivals for the Chinese nation. In recent years, with the rehabilitation and development of traditional culture, people began to attach more value to these native festivals. Quite a few intellectuals have suggested that people should be given a day off on some traditional festivals to show the cultural significance of these festivals. Many businessmen have put forward new ideas in terms of beautifying and developing the traditional festivals as a way to diversify the commodities for festivals catering to people's various needs. For ordinary people, these traditional festivals are precious time for reunion with their family members. Niangao (New Year cakes) for New Year, Tangyuan (dumplings

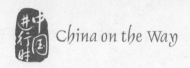

made of glutinous rice flour with fillings) for Lantern Festival, Zongzi (pyramid-shaped dumplings made of glutinous rice wrapped in bamboo or reed leaves) for Dragon Boat Festival, and moon cakes for Mid-autumn Day have become good choices for people to send their greetings and wishes to their relatives and friends. Chinese are enjoying their traditional festivals in a wide variety of ways.

The foreign festivals, such as Christmas, Valentine's Day, Thanksgiving Day, April Fool's Day, Halloween and so on are winning more and more popularity among Chinese, especially the young people. On these foreign festivals, people are strongly attracted by the diversified sorts of gifts available in the supermarkets. Young people would go with friends in twos and threes to enjoy themselves heartily during the festivals. On Christmas Eve of 2006, Beijing became a city of dazzling lights. In the grand hall of the State Guest Hotel, a banquet was held with the theme of "One World, One Christmas". Over a thousand honored guests from home and abroad attended the banquet. In Beijing Concert Hall, a Christmas symphony was being staged while in the pubs in Houhai, many young people were enjoying themselves heartily drinking, singing, and dancing.

However, there are also some people who doubt if the introduction of foreign festivals is really necessary since we have already so many festivals of our own. Actually, the answer is yes. For one thing, the introduction of the foreign festivals provides a good opportunity for Chinese to experience foreign cultures, enriches their lives with rejoicings, promotes cultural exchange and strengthens friendships. For another thing, from the perspective of the businessmen, the introduction of these festivals is instrumental to stimulating domestic consumption and expanding domestic demands.

中国人爱喝茶

　　中国人在日常生活中不可缺少的饮料之一就是茶。俗话说，开门七件事，"柴、米、油、盐、酱、醋、茶"，可见喝茶在中国人生活中的重要性，如同西方人喝咖啡一样。中国人喝茶已有四千多年的历

史，以茶待客是中国人的一种习惯。客人进门，主人立即送上一杯香气扑鼻的茶水，边喝茶边谈话，气氛轻松愉快。

在中国，茶已形成一种独特的文化。人们把煎茶、品茶作为一种艺术。自古至今，中国各地都设有不同形式的茶楼、茶馆等，北京繁华的前门大街旁就有很多特色茶馆。人们在那里，喝茶、吃点心、欣赏文艺演出，可谓休息、娱乐一举两得。在中国南方，不但有茶楼、茶馆，还有茶棚，这种茶棚多设在风景优美的地方，游人一边喝茶一边观景。

喝茶的学问很多。就拿茶叶来说，各地嗜好不同，喜好喝茶的品种也不一样。北京人爱喝花茶，上海人则喜好绿茶，中国东南的福建人却爱喝红茶。有些地方，喝茶时还喜欢往茶里放些佐料，如湖南一些地方常用姜盐茶待客，不仅有茶叶，而且有盐、姜、炒黄豆和芝麻，喝茶时边摇边喝，最后把黄豆、芝麻、姜和茶叶一起倒入口中，慢慢地嚼出香味，所以不少地方又称"喝茶"为"吃茶"。

沏茶的方法各地也有不同的习惯。中国西部一

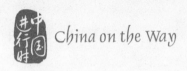

带喜好用大茶壶；中国东部的福建省漳州一带的工夫茶，不仅茶具别具一格，而且沏法也很特别，形成了独特的茶道艺术。

在中国各地，喝茶的礼节也不一样。在北京，主人端上茶来，客人应立即站起来，双手接过茶杯，说声"谢谢"。在南方的广东、广西，主人端上茶后，客人要用右手指弯曲后轻轻地敲三下桌面，以示谢意。在另一些地区，客人想继续喝茶，茶杯中应留些茶水，主人见了会继续加茶水，如果将茶水全部喝完，主人认为你不再喝了，也就不给你加茶水了。

Drinking Teas

Tea is an indispensable beverage in the life of the Chinese people. The significance of tea for Chinese may be expressed by the popular saying that "There are seven things you need for a new day, namely, firewood, rice, cooking oil, salt, sauce, vinegar, and tea." Tea is for Chinese what coffee is for the Westerners. Chinese have been drinking teas for over 4,000 years and it is the tradition to serve tea for guests in China. When a visitor comes, the host would serve a cup of tea with a delicate scent that delights the nose. They will sip the tea when they chat, creating a relaxing and happy atmosphere.

In China, tea has become a particular culture. People consider

making and drinking tea as art. Throughout Chinese history, a great variety of tea shops and tea houses have been established in every part of China. There are many tea houses on both sides of the prosperous Qianmen Street in Beijing. People there can both relax and entertain by drinking tea, eating desserts, and enjoying artistic performances. In the southern China, apart from the tea shops and tea houses, there are tea shelters, which are usually located at places of scenic beauty so that the travelers can enjoy the fascinating views while drinking tea.

The making and drinking of various teas found across China provides an interesting study. Different tastes of people from different areas favor different teas. Beijingers love flower tea; Shanghainese prefer green tea, while Fujianese in the southeast of China favor black tea. In some places, people like to add spices to tea. For example, the southern parts of China like Hunan Province often serve their guests a special tea with salt, ginger, stir-fried soybeans, and sesame. They usually shake the cup while drinking the tea infusion until at long last, they take the soybeans, sesame, ginger, and tea leaves altogether into their mouths, chew them slowly, and enjoy the delicious taste. Thus, "drinking tea" is also called "eating tea" in many places. There are also various types of tea beneficial to the human body and may be used according to a person's health concerns. Additionally, many people may adjust the types of tea they drink according to the change of seasons. For example, people are more likely to drink flower tea in the spring, and believe that green tea is better for the summer, with oolong tea, white tea, and yellow tea considered as more appropriate for the fall, and black tea and dark green tea preferred during winter.

Differences also exist in customs of making teas. In the west of China, people usually prepare a big tea pot. Zhangzhou in Fujian Province, east of China, have invented their own unique way of tea-drinking – Gongfu Tea, unparalled not only in their tea sets, but also in their way of making tea.

People in different areas of China also differ in their drinking customs. In Beijing, when the host serves the tea, the guest should stand up, take the tea cup with both hands, and then say "thank you". In southern China like Guangdong Province and Guangxi Province, after the host serves the tea, the guest is supposed to curve the right-hand fingers and knock softly on the table three times as a token of thanks. In other areas, if the guests want to drink more, they should leave some tea in the teacups so as to inform the hosts of their needs. If they drink all the tea in the teacups, the host would think that they don't want any more and consequently would not serve more.

中国人喝酒的艺术

中国是礼仪之邦，饮酒也可谓历史悠久。中国历史上有关酒的故事很多：晋代诗人陶渊明不能一日无酒；唐代大诗人李白"斗酒诗百篇"，等等。中国古人常把饮酒视为人生最重要的事情之一，智者仁人常常是在"一醉方休"的酒境中彻悟人生的。

饮酒至今，人们虽已不像古人那样，无酒不成诗，可酒仍是人们生活中不可缺少的一部分，是社交礼仪中必不可少的一环。各种宴会、聚餐，酒几乎是不可缺少的，人们常说"无酒不成席"。因此，了解中国的酒，

也就更多地了解了中国人的生活、环境和性情。

　　中国人饮酒讲究一定的礼节。在宴席上，通常以敬酒来表示对主人、长辈、老师或领导的尊重和谢意。敬酒时，可与被敬者亲切碰杯，敬者一般把杯中酒先喝完，以表达诚意。有的地方喝酒还沿袭了传统酒桌游戏，猜拳或行酒令，参与游戏的人，输了就要喝酒。古代读书人行酒令一般是对诗或对联。

　　在礼节上，不胜酒力的人，为了礼貌，也要参与主人的敬酒，可以以茶、果汁代酒，干杯时一定要随大家一齐站起来，酒杯必须触到嘴唇，才算有礼。

　　中国人敬酒时，往往都想让对方多喝点酒，以表示自己尽到了主人之谊。客人喝得越多，主人就越高兴，这说明客人看得起自己；如果客人不喝酒，主人就会觉得有失面子。

一般在酒席开始、主人简短致辞后，便开始了第一次敬酒。这时宾主都要起立，主人先将杯中的酒一饮而尽，并将空酒杯口朝下，说明自己已经喝完，以示对客人的尊重。客人一般也要喝完。在席间，如果酒席不只一桌，主人往往还分别到各桌去敬酒。

然后是"回敬"，即客人向主人敬酒。"回敬"后便开始"互敬"，即客人与客人之间的"敬酒"。为了使对方多饮酒，敬酒者往往会找出各种必须喝酒的理由，若被敬酒者无法找出反驳的理由，就得喝酒。在这种双方寻找论据的同时，感情得到进一步交流。

"代饮"是酒桌上既不失风度、又不使宾主扫兴的饮酒方式。当敬酒者一定要表达对某人的敬意而敬酒时，被敬者不会喝或不能喝时，可请人代酒。代饮酒人一般与他有亲密的关系。在婚礼上，男女双方的伴郎和伴娘往往是代饮的首选人物，故酒量必须大。为了劝酒，酒席上有许多趣话，如"感情深，一口闷；感情厚，喝个够；感情浅，舔一舔"。

"罚酒"也是中国人"敬酒"的一种独特方式。"罚酒"的理由也是五花八门的。最为常见的有对酒席迟到者"罚酒三杯"，有时带点开玩笑的性质。

喝酒是一种享受。一饮而尽也好，慢慢小酌也罢，饮者能够品味酒的醇香，快乐尽兴足已。在宴席上，大家互敬共饮，气氛热烈融洽。中国人的好客，

也在酒席上发挥得淋沥尽致。人与人的感情交流随
着一次次敬酒不断得到升华。

The Chinese Art of Drinking Liquors

China is a land of many traditions. Etiquette is an essential
part of many of these traditions, and even governs the time-honored
history of drinking liquors. Throughout the history of China, there
are many stories about liquors: Tao Yuanming, the renowned poet in
the Jin Dynasty could not go even for one day without liquor; Li Bai,
the well-known and prolific poet of the Tang Dynasty, had a reputation for coming up with hundreds of poems while drinking a jar of
liquor. People in the ancient times used to deem drinking liquor as
one of the most important things in life as it was believed that in-
ebriation allowed great minds to catch the real meaning of life.

Granted, most people no longer drink liquor with quite the
abandon of people in the ancient times. However, liquor remains
an integral part of many people's daily life and an indispensable
component of social intercourse. Liquor is virtually a must for feasts
and gatherings of all kinds. Hence the saying: "A banquet without
liquor is not a real one." Therefore, knowledge of the history and
tradition of Chinese liquors can be of great help for learning the
life, environment, and characteristics of Chinese people.

Chinese have certain routines to observe when drinking liquors.
At a feast, one usually toasts the host, the elder people, the teachers

or the leaders as a sign of one's respect and acknowledgement of their status. When toasting, the toastmaster will often clink glasses softly with the one he or she wants to toast and then drink up the liquor first so as to show his or her sincerity. In some areas, the tradition of playing games at feasts such as finger-guessing games and serving a round of liquor to guests while drinking liquor has been passed down. People involved in the games must drink as a punishment if they lose. In ancient times, intellectuals used to drink liquor in a round by way of matching poems and couplets.

In observance of proper etiquette, even those who can not drink too much should still take part in the toasting activity of the host to show their courtesy. They are allowed to substitute tea or juice for the liquor. When the toastmaster asks for a bottoms-up, even those who choose not to drink liquor are expected to stand with the others and raise their cup to their lips so as to be seen as polite.

When Chinese toast their guests, they want their guests to drink as much as possible showing that they have been responsible hosts. The more the guests drink, the happier the hosts are, because this indicates that the guests respect the hosts. By contrast, if the guests do not drink at all, the hosts would feel shamed.

Generally speaking, at the beginning of the feast, the host would start the first round of toasting after giving a short opening speech. At this time, all the guests are expected to stand, then the host would drink up the liquor in the cup and turn the cup upside down to show that the cup is empty as a sign of respect for the

guests. The guests should also drink up the liquor in their cups. If there is more than one table at the feast, the host would toast the guests at each table, one by one.

Next comes the re-toasting, with the guests toasting the host. After re-toasting comes mutual toasting, referring to toasts among the guests themselves. In order to encourage people to drink more, the toastmaster would rack his or her brain to look for any kind of excuse. If the one being toasted fails to come up with a satisfactory refutation, he or she would have to drink the liquor. It is in the process of looking for excuses that an exchange between the two is promoted.

Drinking for others is a good way that is neither rude nor inconsiderate to the host. When the toastmaster is to express his or her respect for a person, yet the person does not or can not drink liquor, he or she can ask someone to drink for him or her. The person who drinks the liquor for another person often has an intimate relationship with the person. In a wedding ceremony, the best man and the bridesmaid are the first choice for drinking for the newly-weds, and thus they must be able to drink a great deal of liquor. In order to persuade people to drink more liquor, people have coined many witty sayings like "A good relationship requires a gulp in one breath; an intimate relationship entails adequate liquor; even a plain relationship needs a sip".

Another form of toasting for Chinese is to make someone drink as a forfeit. The excuses for such behavior vary. The most ordinary is the "three cups of liquor for late arrivals". Often, this is merely something said in jest.

Drinking liquor is an enjoyment. Be it a gulp in one breath or more leisurely sips, so long as people enjoy themselves by tasting the luscious flavor of liquor, that's enough. In addition, exchange among people tends to be promoted when toasting. At a feast, people toast each other in a pleasant atmosphere, strengthening their relationships among each other. It is at the drinking feasts that the hospitality of Chinese people is on its fullest display.

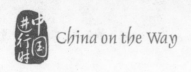

诚信，永远的美德

　　杜海是一家电器公司的销售员。由于刚毕业薪水低，他成了一名"月光（月薪花光）族"。在他的钱包里放着五张各商业银行的信用卡，贷款总额达三万余元。每个月他都会收到至少一家银行的欠账通知单，然后他就从别的银行透支，开始拆东墙补西墙，每次他也总能过关。

　　据统计，近年来中国信用卡发行量突破1000万张，人民币透支近300亿元。不过，随着中国"信用档案"制度的启动，"月光族"的日子将会越来越难过。"信用档案"是个人信用信息的基础数据库，它会如实记录客户原始的信用信息。任何一个人，只要在中国各银行办理了贷款和信用卡，其个人信用信息将由办理银行传递给中国中央银行的信用卡管理部门。中央银行再搭建信用卡个人信息系统平台，供中国所有的银行联网查询。

　　一次失信就会在一段时间内影响个人信用活动，

这和以前有很大区别。信用卡持有人不仅要提供包括姓名、身份证号码、住址、工作单位等基本信息，还要填写住房公积金等附加资料。同时，在中国所有银行的联网中，个人欠账的信息会一笔笔地记录在案。中国还将贯彻国际惯例，借钱不还等负面信息虽不会成为永久的"信用污点"，但一般负面记录将保留七年，破产记录一般保留十年。

在中国传统的交往礼仪中，很讲究诚实守信。诚实，就是忠诚正直，言行一致，表里如一；守信，就是遵守诺言，不虚伪欺诈。

其实早在2000多年前，孔子就教育他的弟子要诚信，一部《论语》中，有23处谈到了"信"的重要。中国千百年流传下来的古话中，如"言必信，行必果"、"一言既出，驷马难追"等都形象地表达了中华民族诚实守信的品质。

虽然大多数的中国人仍以"诚信"为自己做人的原则，但有少数人为了个人私利在破坏着这一古训。因此，"信用档案"制度的启动，代表着中国企业和个人的现代信用体系正走向正轨。现代信用制度的实施，也将使中国人诚实守信的古老传统发扬光大，永不丢失。

Honesty and Trustworthiness— The Never-Lost, Excellent Tradition of China

Du Hai is a salesman at a company selling electric appliances. Having recently graduated from school his salary barely makes ends meet. Inside his wallet are five credit cards issued by five different commercial banks, with a combined balance of 30,000 yuan in debt. He would receive a monthly statement and would borrow from another card to pay off the debt for this account. Amazingly, he has survived these difficulties.

Statistics show that in recent years the circulation of credit cards in China has exceeded 10 million and the overdraft of Renminbi has reached almost 30 billion. However, with the launch of the "credit record" system, life for people like Du Hai would become more and more difficult. The "credit record" is a basic database of personal credit information. It will record the original credit information of the clients honestly. Anyone who has registered for a loan or a credit card at the banks would have his or her personal credit information delivered by the bank to the credit management department of the Central Bank of China. The Central Bank of China is building a database for personal credit information so that all banks in China can have access to the information through the Internet.

A failure in trust once would have a negative impact on personal credit activities for a period of time. This differs greatly from the previous system. Currently, credit card holders not only need to provide basic information including their names, ID Card numbers, addresses, and employment information, but they are also required to provide additional information such as their housing accumulation funds, etc. Meanwhile, the debt information will also be recorded one by one clearly on the Internet, available for all banks in China. Additional changes include adherence to international routines that provide time limits to the duration of negative credit information held against an individual as the result of not paying his or her debts in a timely manner. Ordinary negative records will be kept for at least 7 years while a record of bankruptcy will be kept for 10 years. This will serve to improve the serious overdraft situation in the national banking industry.

According to Chinese tradition of social intercourse, great importance has been attached to the quality of being honest and keeping one's promise. Being honest means being faithful and righteous, and saying what one thinks deep down. Keeping one's promise refers to carrying out one's promise and not cheating others.

As a matter of fact, over 2000 years ago, Confucius had already told his disciples to be honest and keep their promises. The significance of "keeping one's promise" is touched upon 23 times in the single book of *Analects of Confucius*. The Chinese characteristic of being honest and keeping one's promise can also been seen vividly from the ancient mottos that have been passed down such as "keep your promises and carry them out immediately", "what one has said can never be unsaid", etc.

Although most Chinese today still adhere to the principle of being honest and keeping one's promises, there are also a few people breaking from this tradition for their personal benefit. The launch of the "credit record" system is an indication that the modern credit system for enterprises and individuals is becoming more and more complete. The establishment of the modern credit system will promote the ancient Chinese tradition of being honest and keeping one's promises as well.

国学"大餐"变"快餐"

近一两年，中央电视台的《百家讲坛》栏目捧红了不少学者明星，收视率、覆盖面数以百万、千万计，从厦门大学教授易中天的《品三国》到学者阎崇年、隋丽娟的《讲清史》、《说慈禧》，一个比一个火暴。特别是2006年国庆节和2007年春节期间，北京师范大学年轻教授于丹开讲的《论语心得》、《庄子心得》更是盛况空前，收视率达数千万人次。由此出版的《于丹论语心得》、《于丹庄子心得》书籍也带来了轰动效应，创造了惊人的销售业绩，销售量达到了上百万册。

电视传播效应不仅让几位明星学者迅速走红，受到大众追捧，还带来了传统国学热在普通民众中的迅速升温。对此"国学快餐"文化现象，社会舆论评说不一，喜忧参半。

在忧者看来，"国学快餐"不能让人们扎扎实实地阅读和理解经典，把握国学精髓，让国学成为人们

道德取向的基础。用"国学快餐"的形式来传播国学，非但不能重振国学，反而有可能使国学庸俗化、简单化、娱乐化，得便宜的只是少部分人的腰包，输的却可能是整个民族的人文精神。

在当前这个快节奏时代，太多东西被"快餐化"了，从日常饮食、学位文凭，到恋爱结婚等等，各类"快餐"充斥着浮躁的社会。甚至连最后一块严肃、庄重的国学阵地也都"快餐化"了。如此"传统国学大倾销"，其产品媚俗浅陋，非国学之本源与精华，误导了大众。

而喜者认为，大众需要亲近国学。在现代生活快节奏下，人们的文化消费往往是通过电视、网络和畅销书籍这类大众文化载体来实现的。"国学快餐"就是国学经典的"通俗化"。就像网友们所说，国学经典是不好消化的豆粒，"国学快餐"则是容易吸收的美味豆腐。

"国学快餐"的流行象征着时代民意的胜利，改变了国学经典尘封于图书馆和寄生于学术的高高在上的地位，打破了文化界独品的学术特权，打通了人人共享国学文化的渠道。于丹等学者传播的"国学快餐"，恰恰汲取了传统国学中的智慧，形成对现代人思想启迪和为人处世的"道"，具有现实意义。"国学快餐"作为传统国学的"现代文化创造"，说不定将来也会成为经典。"国学快餐"使传统"国学"迅速

普及，受到当代大众如此青睐，无疑是一件利国利民、利于弘扬中华民族传统文化的大好事。

Public Craze for Ancient Classics

Since 2006, "Lecture Room", a program shown on China Central Television, has made many scholars known overnight, and the program's ratings are sky-rocketing.

Among these star scholars are Professor Yi Zhongtian of Wuhan University who talks about the Three Kingdoms, and Yan Chongnian and Sui Lijuan who are known respectively for expounding the history of the Qing Dynasty and the back-seat Manchu ruler Empress Dowager Cixi.

During the 2006 National Day and the 2007 Spring Festival, Yu Dan, a professor with Beijing Normal University, was viewed by millions as she expounded her understanding of two Chinese classics: *Analects of Confucius* and *Book of Zhuang Zi*. The broadcast was an exceptional hit. Her books on the same topics published soon afterward were also bestsellers and set a record, selling several million copies.

While making the scholars known overnight, TV's broad viewing audience also triggers the public's interest in Chinese classics. However, the style and format of the presentation have led to a measure of controversy. Some praise, and some criticize.

Those in the opposition camp believe this style of presentation is the equivalent of "fast food", providing a quick and easy overview without encouraging the viewers to read the ancient classics or learn the essence on which to build their morality. Instead of spreading and reviving Chinese classics, it degrades the classics into kitsch, a simple entertainment. In the end, only a few will benefit financially from the success of the programs, to the detriment of the cultural spirit of the entire nation.

In today's fast-moving, blundering society, too many things have been turned into "fast food". From daily food and cram classes to speed dating and flash marriage, various "fast food style" activities are taking place every day. Now we see the latest offence: the originally serious study of cultural classics is being packed into a sleazy commercialized product, misleading the general public.

But the supporters hold that this format offers the public an appropriate approach to the classics. In a fast-changing world, people learn and enjoy culture by way of mass media like TV, the Internet and bestsellers. Turning the classics into cultural "fast food" is the best way to make them popular and easy to understand. As some netizens say, the classics are like indigestible peas, and now they are made into tofu.

The popularity of "fast food style" classics is a victory for the mass audience. It shakes the lofty status of the classics, often held dust-laden in libraries and confined only to academia, smashes the invisible privilege of a small number of people, and makes them accessible to the public. What Yu Dan and others do is to provide

practical guidance by associating the wisdom of the classics with current life.

It's still early to predict if such a cultural creation will become classics in their own right. What we can say is that it has revived the popularity of the classics within a short time. From this perspective, it is providing a great service carrying forward traditional Chinese culture.

姚明——中国人的骄傲

姚明出生于中国上海的一个篮球世家。这个2米26的巨人，2002年进入美国休斯顿火箭队后，从此展开了他不同寻常的NBA生涯。如今的他已从一个菜鸟成长为一名真正让对手畏惧的NBA超级中锋，而中间的辛酸和坎坷历程只有他自己知道，用他的队友肖恩·巴蒂尔的话说："如果不依靠刻苦训练，没有人会因为经常观看EPSN的精彩进球集锦而成为统治者的。"经过多年在美国的摸爬滚打，他用刻苦和幽默征服了NBA，同样也征服了中国篮球爱好者的心。

在中国，他可谓家喻户晓，拥有一大批铁杆球迷。他有典型的东方人性格，不温不火，大度谦逊，上进心强，集体观念良好。从未见过他在球场上与别人发生争执，更别说大打出手。就算面对对方的挑衅，他也能够保持冷静。在球场上他也是无私的，经常为对友挡、拆、传球。

说实话，要做一名优秀的篮球运动员，姚明的身

体条件还不够完美，他的臂展短，弹跳力和爆发力差，身体对抗性不强，移动慢，体力差，根本无法和黑人和欧洲人媲美。他唯一的优势就是那2米26的

身高！他能取得今天的成就完全靠自己坚持不懈的努力。队友说他每天来得最早，却是最晚一个走的！正是这样的刻苦，使姚明变得强壮了，技术全面，防守积极，中投命中率颇高！在一次比赛中，他曾经21投15中，命中率72%，罚球命中率在90%以上。这就是姚明通过努力换来的成果！

目前，NBA与中国的电视合作伙伴已增至24家。而在去年转播的270场比赛中，69%的赛事是火箭队的比赛。铺天盖地的报道让火箭队成为中国球迷最为喜欢的球队。作为一名中国人，姚明在美国电视的上镜率最高，几乎天天出现。他创造了太多的第一，他的每个进步都令中国人感到由衷地高兴。

2007年夏天，姚明结婚了。他像普通上海人一样到苏州为新娘订婚纱，到杭州拍婚纱照，然后挑了8月6日这个黄道吉日，在上海的一家五星级酒店举办婚宴，邀请的亲朋好友只有9桌。一个世界级的篮球明星，其婚礼还不如一些普通上海人的婚礼来得排场，这也正是姚明的魅力所在，他为人低调，不爱张扬和铺张。

姚明是中国人的骄傲。在美国，人们已经对这个中国人有着前所未有的尊敬，没人敢小视他，就连对手和那些原来不看好姚明的专家也对他刮目相看，一些不愿意承认姚明实力的教练、EPSN评论家们甚至对这个中国巨人褒奖有佳。

一位在休斯顿的华侨说道："你们知道吗？在火箭队的主场，每一次姚明有精彩表现的时候，球迷都会疯狂地站起来高呼姚明的名字，举着写有姚明标语的牌子，穿着印有11号的火箭队球衣，唱着《姚之歌》。主场的评论员也在姚明每次得分后用拉长的语调重复姚明的名字。"

在异国他乡，姚明代表的不仅仅是火箭队，他代表了海内外的中国人！中国人为姚明而骄傲！全世界的人也通过姚明更多地认识和了解了中国人，或者说不断改变着对中国人的看法！

Yao Ming — The Pride of Chinese

Yao Ming was born into a family of basketball players in Shanghai, China. The 2.26 meter-high giant joined the Houston Rockets, U.S. in 2002, hence embarking on his spectacular career in the NBA. Today's Yao Ming has grown from an unknown to a formidable NBA super-center. Yet the tears and sweat he has shed during the process were barely known. Shane Battier, his team-mate remarked, "You must practice hard. No one can become such a success in the court by simply watching the video collections of excellent scores of EPSN." After years of perseverance, Yao Ming has conquered NBA as well as Chinese basketball fans with his diligence and humor.

In China, Yao Ming is a household name with many devoted

fans. He has inherited typical Chinese characteristics – calm nature, humility, enterprising spirit, and cooperative attitude. He has never been seen quarrelling with anyone on the court, let alone fighting. Even if someone tried to find fault with him, he would always remain calm. He is also selfless on the court – sharing plays with his teammates and passing the ball (mostly to Tracy McGrady) rather than keeping the focus on himself.

Frankly speaking, for having such success as a basketball player, Yao Ming is far from being perfect physically, referring to his short arms, dissatisfactory springing capability, lack of aggressiveness, slow movement and limited strength. Viewing from this respect, Yao Ming cannot match many of his counterparts. His only natural advantage is his 2.26 meters height. His success today is entirely due to his persistent efforts. His roommates said that he was always the first to get up in the morning and the last to leave the court. It is his dedication to hard practice day after day that has built his strong body and improved his skills. Yao Ming now can take dominance when defending the ball, and his chances of scoring have become extremely good. Once in a match, he scored 15 out of 21 attempts, with a scoring rate of 72% and his rate for converting free throws is over 90%. This is Yao Ming's "gain" after his "pain".

At present, the NBA has established cooperation with 24 TV stations in China. Of the 270 basketball matches broadcast last year, 69% were the Rockets'. Covering so many of the Rockets' games has not only made the team the most popular among Chinese basketball fans, but also enabled Yao Ming, a Chinese player, to appear on TV in the United States almost every day. He has set numerous records in the field. All Chinese are exhilarated by Yao Ming's success and strides forward.

In the summer of 2007, Yao Ming got married. Like an ordinary Shanghainese, he went to Suzhou to order the wedding dress for his bride, picked the propitious date of August 6th, and held the wedding banquet in a five-star hotel in Shanghai on that day. All the relations and friends invited were seated at no more than nine tables. As a world-famous basketball star, his wedding ceremony was no more luxurious than that of some ordinary Shanghainese, showing Yao Ming's desire to keep a low profile and maintain a frugal lifestyle.

Yao Ming is the pride of Chinese. In the United States, people have shown unprecedented respect for him and no one dares underestimate him. Even his opponents and those experts who used to look down upon him had to change their opinions. Even the coaches and EPSN critics who had been reluctant to recognize Yao Ming's capabilities lavish their praises on him now.

An American-Chinese in Houston said, "You know what? Each time Yao Ming presented an excellent performance at the Rockets home matches, his fans would stand yelling out his name hysterically, holding posters of Yao Ming in their hands, wearing Rockets' clothes printed 11, and sing heartily 'The Song of Yao'. Every time when Yao Ming scored in the home matches, the commentators would repeat Yao Ming's name again and again in a deliberately prolonged voice."

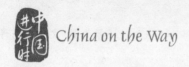

In foreign countries, Yao Ming does not simply stand for the Houston Rockets, he also represents Chinese people both at home and abroad. Chinese people take pride in Yao Ming as he has become a model by whom people all over the world have learned more about Chinese people, constantly changing their previous perceptions.

第三篇
社会与发展
SOCIETY & DEVELOPMENT

中国百姓期待"幸福指数"

穷书生 富书生

大学毕业了，当村官去！

挡不住的中国房价

中国女性更自信了

大学生从"精英"走向"大众"

中国百姓期待"幸福指数"

2006年,中国国家统计局宣布,中国将推出幸福指数的统计内容,政府将把"幸福指数"作为衡量国家协调发展的一项指标。

各个媒体随之呼应,有关"幸福"的调查和讨论层出不穷,例如"富人的幸福感比不上穷人","农民幸福感最强","中国幸福指数位居全球第31位,远高于日本、韩国、新加坡"等等。时下"幸福"成了一个热门字眼。

根据中国国家统计局的解释,"幸福

指数"用来反映普通百姓对自己的生活条件，包括收入、就业、保障的满意度以及对自然环境的感受。

北京理工大学研究中国问题的胡星斗教授说："幸福应当是包括很多方面的，如社会稳定、犯罪率较低、人均住房适宜、医疗状况、受教育状况良好，甚至包括人均绿地面积不断提高等，'幸福指数'应是一个综合指数。"

还有市民表示，除了一些基本的生活条件外，精神方面得到满足也很重要。北京思源社会科学研究中心总裁就表示，"幸福指数"对不同状况的人有不同的结构性要求。他心目中的'幸福指数'应该包括能够从事自己喜爱的、且对社会有意义的工作，能够自由表达个人对于社会的看法、建议和要求，并真正感受到做这一切所带来的变化。这对他来说是最大的幸福。

而一位知名网评人则发表不同意见说，居民收入增长减缓，致使居民对物价上涨的感受增强，同时面临就业压力、医疗费用上涨、教育投资加大、巨额房贷等重重压力，"幸福指数"如何将所有内容包括其中呢？

仁者见仁，智者见智。但无论怎样，对普通大众来说，"幸福指数"的推出应是一件好事，我们也应该理智看待它：考察"幸福指数"，并不是追求它无限增长，而是力求通过它来考察普通群众的主观生

活质量状况和变化趋势，进而调整政策取向，促进社
会发展和社会良性运转。

Chinese Commoners Are Expecting the "Happiness Index"

In 2006, the State Statistics Bureau of China declared that China would bring forward the results of the "happiness index", which would be used to measure the harmonious development of the state.

With the mass media echoing, investigations and discussions concerning "happiness" emerged in an endless stream. For instance, investigations show that "happiness of the rich is no match for that of the poor", that "Chinese farmers feel the happiest", or that "China ranks 31st in the world in terms of the happiness index, much higher than Japan, South Korea and Singapore."

According to the State Statistics Bureau of China, the "happiness index" is used to demonstrate how people feel about their living conditions, including their income, employment, social security and the natural environment.

Professor Hu Xingdou, who researches various Chinese issues at the Beijing Institute of Engineering, said, "Happiness should cover many aspects, such as social stability, a low crime rate, adequate *per capita* housing, appropriate medical care, good education, and even suitable *per capita* green ways and natural areas. The

'happiness index' is an integrated result of evaluations such as these."

Some urban residents hold the view that apart from basic living conditions, mental satisfaction is also of great significance. According to the president of the Beijing Siyuan Social Sciences Research Center, the "happiness index" has different structural demands for those in various conditions. To his mind, the "happiness index" should include the ability to work at a joyful and meaningful job, the ability to freely express one's views and suggestions towards society, and the feeling of genuine experience with respect to the corresponding changes. He believes that the achievement of all these would give him a sense of the greatest happiness.

A well-known Internet commentator, however, argued that slow income growth added to the rate of economic inflation is causing increased pressure with respect to one's employment. Also of concern are rising medical costs, increasing costs for education, and large numbers of housing loans. He suggests that it is difficult for the "happiness index" to cover these aspects of life confronting the population.

Opinions vary from individual to individual. While the name "happiness index" provides a pleasant feeling, it is important to understand the purpose behind the investigation of the "happiness index". Rather than simply providing an index from which to pursue an endless rise, the endeavor provides a tool to investigate the common people's subjective life quality and its tendency, for the purpose of adjusting relevant policies and promoting the harmonious development and healthy operation of society.

穷书生　富书生

　　经过改革开放和市场经济洗礼的中国知识分子，正在迅速成长为中国新的富裕阶层。

　　中国有两句古话，叫做"君子固穷"、"学而优则仕"，意思是君子善于忍受贫穷，学业出众就会踏上仕途，这表明中国古代知识分子经常徘徊在贫困和仕途之间，现在这两句话对于中国知识分子已经不再适用了。

　　据估算，包括大学教授、作家、艺术家在内，中国社会目前共有3800万专业知识分子，其中有1000万人在民营企业工作或者自己开公司，积累着个人财富。继早期的个体户、乡镇企业家、中间商、不动产经营商和贸易商、民营企业家之后，中国正迎来了第六代富裕集体——知识分子阶层。他们中的大部分人都是拥有硕士、博士学位的青年或中年人，出生于20世纪六七十年代，青年时代经历了市场经济的洗礼，在改革开放的黄金时期迎来了人生最美好的时

光，具有非凡的商业头脑。

中国社科院社会学研究所位副研究员李春玲说："在中国传统文化中，知识分子多集中在人文科学领域，而现在工程、经济等专业技术人员也加入进来，他们共同构成了中国当代知识分子阶层。"

20世纪80年代末、90年代初，中国的知识分子多直接下海经商，比如自己开办公司。这是他们将知识转化为财富的最初方式。现在，知识分子更多地选择了将自己的知识转化为知识产权，将科研项目转化为产品，出售给公司，而非亲自下海。比如在企业做兼职、任顾问或独立董事；或者带领自己的研究生为企业做与其专业相关的项目。

35岁的北京大学法学博士胡戎恩属于典型的创业型知识分子，曾任上海政法学院的立法学教师。此前他还当了五年法官，辞职后回到家乡温州创办小型水电站，挖到了第一桶金。后来胡戎恩成立了上海欧晟置业有限公司，主要从事各类房地产开发和管理。胡先生尽管忙于企业经营，但一直醉心学术研究。他认为："有了钱可以让人更自信，更独立。"他致富后的理想是贤者云集，切磋学问。

此外，在中国知识致富人群中还有许多人依靠专业知识，或成为职业经理人，或成为金融机构的经济分析师。另有一些知识分子以"卖文"为生，为报纸、杂志撰稿，收益也颇丰。随着中国经济的崛起，

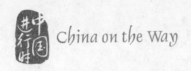

中国的"儒商"正以其智慧创造并积累着财富。

Chinese Intellectuals:
No Longer Poor Scholars

Two Chinese proverbs, "a man of moral integrity shall endure poverty" and "a good scholar can make an official" reveal ancient scholars' dilemma as to whether to endure poverty or to take an official career. But these sayings no longer apply to today's scholars. Intellectuals are growing into China's new middle class thanks to the introduction of reform and opening-up and the market economy.

It's said that China has 38 million professionals including professors, writers and artists. Of them, 10 million are accumulating personal wealth by running businesses or working for non-state-owned enterprises. Including individual households, township entrepreneurs, middlemen, real estate developers, non-state-owned business managers, etc. the sixth-generation nouveau riche is taking shape in China. Most of these are young or middle-aged, with a master's or a doctoral degree. Born in the 1960s, they have undergone the test of the market economy, and have shown brilliant talent in financial matters. Now is the prime time in their lives.

Li Chunling, associate research fellow of the Institute of Sociology under the Chinese Academy of Social Sciences, says, "Traditionally, Chinese intellectuals mainly engage in humane

studies, and now, engineering and economic professionals are join-
ing them to make up the new intellectual stratum."

In the late 1980s and early 1990s, intellectuals often chose to
open their own business. Now, they prefer to turn their knowledge
into intellectual property rights or turn scientific research projects
into products and sell them to businesspeople. They often work
part-time as consultants or independent directors, or instructing students on relevant projects for enterprises.

Hu Rongen, 35, is a typical intellectual upstart. The Ph. D in
law of Peking University and judge of five years had once taught
law at Shanghai Institute of Political Science and Law. Later, he
resigned and opened a small hydraulic power station in his hometown of Wenzhou, Zhejiang Province. That was his first barrel of
gold. Then Hu started Shanghai Sundee Group Co. Ltd. and en-
gaged in real estate development and management. As busy as he
is in his business endeavors, his interest in academic research has
never faded. "Earning money can ensure one's independence," he
says. His dream is that with no worry about money, he could invite
a number of his peers to consult and exchange views on academic
issues.

There are also those who act as professional managers or
analysts of financial organizations, and those who live on their con-
tributions to newspapers or magazines. Along with China's economic rise, the scholars-turned businesspeople are creating and
accumulating wealth with their knowledge.

大学毕业了，当村官去！

　　中国大学生正在重新走进农村。迄今为止，中国共有三次知识分子回归农村热潮。20世纪20年代，为改造混乱的农村环境，知识分子开展拯救农村运动；建国后，为建设社会主义新农村，知识分子大规模下放农村。此次大学生下乡则掀起中国知识分子第三次回归农村热潮。正值中国大力推进新农村建设，大学生下乡自然备受关注。

　　2006年，北京市政府公开招聘在郊区农村工作的大学生公务员——村官，协助村长负责农村开发。此次招聘会共有1200余名大学生参加了应聘。通过审核和面试，共选出60名村官，他们被分配到平谷和延庆等地的农村就职。

　　北京市政府计划继续接收村官志愿者的申请，并提供2000个岗位。市政府一名负责人表示，市里正积极探讨吸引大学生参加农村建设的方案，拟根据村官的工作成绩，不断扩大他们的工作范围，最终

将村官队伍扩至8000人。

　　大学生当村官在中国还是一个新现象，它刚一出现，全国各地就纷纷效仿，目前已呈扩大趋势。北京招收的这些大学生村官所学的专业都是农村建设需要的。北京一名村干部介绍说："来我们这里的大学生的专业是果树栽培，这非常有助于村里的果树种植。村民们还向他们学习网上销售，对促进我村的水果销售也有很多好处。"大学生村官利用其专业知识为所在村的发展起到了积极的推动作用。同时，近年来就业岗位增加缓慢，大学生面临就业难问题，选拔村官还可以增加就业岗位。目前中国把农村建设放在重要位置，因此大学生村官将大有用武之地。

Grads Turned Village Heads

Chinese college graduates are turning their eyes to villages. Previously, there have been two waves of intellectuals heading to rural areas. The first was in 1920s when patriotic intellectuals launched a movement to change the chaotic conditions in rural China. The second was after the People's Republic of China was founded in 1949. A large number of intellectuals were sent to build a socialist countryside. The current craze catches wide attention as it also coincides with China's current endeavors to build a new socialist countryside.

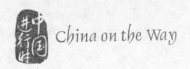

In 2006, Beijing announced recruitment of college graduates for positions working with the leaders of certain suburban villages. Of more than 1,200 grads who applied, 60 passed the examinations and interviews. They were dispatched to Pinggu and Yanqing to assist the village heads in local development.

More applicants are welcome, as Beijing plans to expand the program. A municipal government spokesman says that they're working on attractive policies to engage a total of 8,000 village heads with college education. The grads' performances will be judged and their scope of work will be correspondingly expanded.

While it's still a new practice to select grads as village heads, Beijing is not alone, as the program soon inspired similar efforts across the country.

The grads selected have the skills and knowledge needed by the villages. "The grad working in our village has learned fruit tree planting. He can help us grow fruit trees. He also teaches us online sale, so that we can sell more of our fruits," a village head says, "The grads can use their knowledge to help us. They play a positive role in rural areas." The sluggish job market has made job-hunting difficult in recent years. The villages now offer the grads an opportunity to display their talents, as rural development has become a national priority in present day China.

挡不住的中国房价

　　随着建筑业的繁荣，中国建材市场也日益火暴。一家进入中国不久的外资建材商场已经接待了 3000 万人次的中国顾客。跟欧美一些国家相比，中国的建材并不太贵，但在中国买房后的装修总支出却是相当高的。

　　古梁是一位在北京工作的四川人，他新买的住房价格是85万元，装修却花了10万元。其实，这在中国是普遍的现象：装修费用一般都在买房费用的10%以上，估计一般在12%～20%之间。而在欧美，这个费用应该是5%～10%。

　　中国装修费用高的原因在于中国买家拿到的房子基本上处于"毛坯状态"。古梁带记者到他的新房去看，那里就是水泥墙、水泥地，什么都要"装"上去。而在欧美，"粗装修"一般已经含在房价里。即使是二手的房子，多半也是在墙、地装修后出售的。

　　这两年中国的房价上翻了好几倍。北京、上海等大城市的房价已经远远高于欧美很多同类城市了，如果考虑实际币值因素，可能高出几倍、几十倍都不止。就以上海为例，上海市中心的新房，每平方米价格大约在2万至3.5万元人民币之间。而像德国杜塞尔多夫、科隆这些房价最高的城市，即使在黄金地段，2000欧元（合人民币约21000多元）以上一平方米的房子也是极为罕见的。

　　据有关专家分析，中国房价飞涨的因素，归纳起来大概有几方面：一是银行贷款容易，只要能找到合适的土地，开发商不愁没有资金周转；二是人民币的币值普遍认为被低估，看好这一点，许多境外人士勇敢地把钱投到中国房地产业里去了；三是中国从"公房社会"转向"私房社会"的过程远远没有结束；四

是中国人口城市化进程可能需要上百年时间才能基本完成，住房的供应对象源源不断，而房子越来越少，越来越昂贵，因此人们愿为"自己的天空"倾其所有的想法会更加强烈。

Skyrocketing Housing Prices

China's prospering building industry has boosted its building materials market. The 30 million visitors received by a foreign-funded store of building materials soon after it opened for business is good proof of this. The Chinese pay much less on building materials than the Europeans and Americans, but considerably more on remodeling their new houses.

Gu Liang, a Sichuan native, now works in Beijing. He recently bought a house at 850,000 yuan, and spent another 100,000 yuan remodeling it. This is not rare in China, as the general expense on remodeling accounts for 12-20% of the total cost of a house. The ratio in Europe and America is 5-10%.

Why such a high remodeling expense? Because most of China's new houses are "roughcast". Everything has to be added to the cement walls and cement floors, as Gu Liang did. But in Europe and America, houses are finished before being sold. It's generally the same with second-hand ones.

In the past two years, the cost of Chinese houses has soared

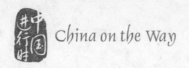
several fold. The housing prices in Beijing, Shanghai and other major cities are much higher than those in Europe and America. Allowing for the appreciation of Renminbi, the gap may be several times or even dozens of times. Take Shanghai for example. New downtown houses are often priced at 20,000-35,000 yuan per square meter, or even higher. But in Dusseldorf and Cologne, cities with the most expensive houses in Europe, it's hard to find houses demanding 2,000-euro (21,000 yuan) per square meter, even in the most expensive areas.

According to experts, four causes have contributed to the rocketing housing prices:

The first is the easy access of bank loans. If the developers can find available land, there is no worry about the capital for development. Secondly, Believing Renminbi has been underestimated, overseas investors are eager to grasp this chance and put money in China's real estate sector. Thirdly, China's shift from government-born houses to individual-born houses is far from being over, and the government is working out one measure after another against building houses at the expense of government departments, thus forcing many urbanites to spend whatever they have to buy a home for themselves. Fourthly, China's urbanization process may last more than 100 years, which means there will remain an endless queue of house purchasers.

中国女性更自信了

　　李曼和她的男友杨杰同在北京一家会计事务所工作，最近正在准备婚礼。杨杰说，结婚的地点、方式等事宜皆由未婚妻做主。他们这种想法和做法在城市年轻男女中很普遍。这从一个侧面表明，婚姻家

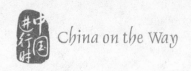

庭中的中国女性地位越来越高，她们有相当的自主权，可以独立决定家庭事务。婚后也决不会做那种逆来顺受的旧式媳妇，而是自主决定是工作还是辞职、生不生小孩等。

随着中国女性经济能力的提高，社会对夫妻间平等话题的讨论持续深入，加上中国社会男女比例失调，中国女性得到了争取自身地位和权益的好机会。一些学者指出，50多年来，中国女性正处在保障自身权益的风口浪尖上。

在城市，年轻人交往更开放，家长制的影响已逐渐减弱，女性在这一过程中表现得更加自信。有学者说，中国的家长制是封建社会的糟粕，它主要与人们赖以生存的土地有关，而城市文化表现的是流动性，女性的才智更能发挥出来。

许多有抱负的女性，即使在婚后也想不断发展自己。许多女性现在努力工作以使自己能在经济上独立，她们不想埋没自己的价值。中国社会科学院学者李银河指出，事实上，有工作的女性为中国家庭的餐桌带来了丰盛的食品，更为明显的是，越来越多的女孩考上大学，且大都名列前茅并从事白领工作。同为中国社会科学院学者的董智颖说，"在许多领域里，女性比男性干得更出色。一些男性也明显感觉到，中国女性更独立、更自信了，她们比从前拥有了更多权利。"

中国政府的确在许多方面实行了男女平等的政策，女性在升学、就业、提职、加薪等方面享有和男子平等的权利。

Chinese Women:
Confident and Independent

Li Man and her boyfriend Yang Jie are working for an accounting firm in Beijing. These days, they're preparing for their wedding. Yang Jie says that all the wedding plans will be decided by Li Man.

This has become the "rule" among young urbanites. It tells the enhanced status of modern Chinese women in marriage and family life. Unlike their mothers, grandmothers or great-grandmothers in feudal China, women today are no longer traditional obedient daughters-in-law. On the contrary, they are quite independent, and can decide on their own family affairs such as whether to work or resign or to have a baby or not.

As women become economically independent, there are more discussions on the equality between husband and wife. The disproportion between numbers of Chinese men and women offers women an excellent opportunity to gain independence and protect their rights and interests. In fact, as some scholars put it, they're enjoying the best chance in more than 50 years.

Perhaps as a result of China's swift growth in recent years,

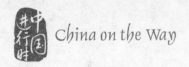

paternalism is fading out, and young urbanites in particular are free to attend social activities, and women gain more confidence. To some scholars, paternalism is the dross of feudal China, and it is closely associated with the land on which people survive. But urban culture has a flowing character, thus giving full play to women's talent.

Marriage can't confine aspiring women if they want to continue self-development. Not wanting to efface themselves, intellectual women work hard to secure economic independence. Working women bring home delicious food, and more and more girls are enrolled in colleges and getting white-collar jobs for their excellent performances, points out Li Yinhe, a scholar with the Chinese Academy of Social Sciences. Dong Zhiying, another scholar from Ms. Li's Academy, notes that women surpass men in many fields, and many men agree that Chinese women are more independent, more confident, and have more power than ever before.

The Chinese government practices a policy of equality between men and women, and women enjoy a level playing field with men regarding college enrollment, employment, promotion and salary raise.

中国富人趋向年轻化

  万事达卡国际组织对北京、上海和广州三大城市的富裕阶层进行调查。他们挑选了300名家庭年收入在1.6万美元和5万美元之间及以上的受访者，其中大部分人（67.1%）年龄低于40岁且受过高等教育，66.9%的人至少拥有学士学位，有25%的人年收入高于5万美元。

  由此看出，中国内地的富裕阶层年轻化的特点十分突出。而相比较，日本的富裕阶层70%以上年龄超过45岁，菲律宾的这一比例为95%，而中国内地只有14%。万事达卡国际组织亚太区首席经济顾问就此分析说，有三方面的原因造就了中国的年轻富人们。首先是外国对华直接投资增长迅猛，涌现了一大批就职于跨国企业的白领；其次，国有企业改革后，提高了对高级专业人才和职业经理人的待遇；此外，中国私营经济蓬勃发展，产生了很多成功的私人企业家。

调查还显示出，中国富人拥有至少一套以上的房产，2004年26%的富人拥有3套房产，8%的人甚至有4套。中国富人购买房产主要是用于投资。随着中国金融市场的发展，越来越多的富人也选择其他金融工具进行投资，如股票、基金、黄金、期货等，房产不再是他们唯一的投资渠道。

中国的富裕阶层相当重视家庭生活。他们认为"拥有幸福家庭是人生中最重要的事情"，若以5分为满分来计算，其获得的分数为4.46；他们"希望尽可能花时间陪伴家人"的意愿强烈，分数为4.19。然而他们也认可"为了工作与事业发展，有时必须牺牲与家人相处的休闲时间"，其分数为2.61。

中国内地的富裕阶层热心公益，73.6%的人愿意支持公益活动，38.9%的人支持环境保护活动。参与其他公益活动的比例分别是：献血（29.6%）、担任志愿者（21.8%）及参与文化遗产的保护工作（8.2%）。39.5%的中国内地富裕阶层表示他们有持续投入公益活动及环境保护的计划，但还有一大部分的富裕阶层尚未决定。

The Young Rich

A survey conducted by MasterCard International of rich urbanites showed that 67.1% were younger than 40, 66.9% had college

or higher education, and 25% had an annual income exceeding US$50,000. The survey included 300 respondents in Beijing, Shanghai and Guangzhou, three major cities of China, whose annual family income ranged from US$16,000 to more than US$50,000.

The survey proved China's rich mainlanders are younger compared with their counterparts in other countries: 70% of the rich in Japan are older than 45, and the ratio is 95% in the Philippines, but in China, only 14% are older than 45.

According to an Asia-Pacific chief economic analyst at MasterCard International, there are three reasons so many young people have broken into the ranks of the rich. The first is soaring overseas investment in China, which has produced a large number of white-collar employees working for the multinationals. The second is the reform of state-owned enterprises, resulting in tremendous increases in the salaries of senior professionals and managers. The last is the flourishing private economy, which explains the handsome incomes of many self-employed managers.

The survey also revealed that most rich Chinese own at least one house each. In 2004, 26% of them had three houses and 8% even owned four. To them, this is one investment tool of many. As the financial market expands, they are turning to other tools such as stocks, mutual funds, gold and futures.

Family life is highly valued by the rich Chinese in general. On a scale of 1 to 5, they scored 4.46 for "regarding a happy family the most important thing in life", and 4.19 for "hoping to stay with

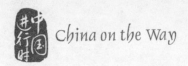

the family as much as possible". But they also agreed that sometimes they had to spend their spare time on work or business, instead of staying with the family, and for this, their score was 2.61.

Other results of the survey indicated 73.6% of the rich support public-welfare activities and 38.9% support environmental protection. Other activities they'd like to undertake include blood donation (29.6%), volunteerism (21.8%), and protection of cultural relics (8.2%). 39.5% of them would continue their support of such activities.

中西快餐斗法中国

　　从本土企业到国际公司，都在角逐中国快餐市场。麦当劳、肯德基等洋快餐店在中国兴起，各类中式快餐、自助餐也吸引了不少食客。肯德基公司一直致力于全力营造符合中国国情的新快餐；"真功夫"和"大娘水饺"两家中式快餐进军北京前，都在上海等南方城市建立了稳固的根据地；"永和豆浆"、"马兰拉面"等分别找到了来自海外的合作伙伴，正在中

国遍地开花。

　　各快餐企业频繁地在中国布局，大家看中的是什么呢？中国烹饪协会的数据显示，目前全国快餐连锁经营网点100万个，年营业额达1800亿元人民币，占全部餐饮业的22%和20%，快餐企业占年度餐饮百强企业的三分之一。业界人士分析，随着人们生活节奏的加快，中国快餐市场将呈现快速发展的势头。

　　但近几年中国超重和肥胖者数量剧增，许多健康专家把其归咎于"洋快餐文化"。一些西式快餐经营者毫不讳言：消费者对西式快餐食品营养的疑虑逐渐成为其继续发展的障碍，赢得消费者的信任已经成为洋快餐迫在眉睫的问题。

　　中国人对健康养生的推崇由来已久，对快餐的营养需求也将加大。中式快餐正在学习西式快餐的管理经验，洋快餐也在借鉴中餐的烹饪技巧以适应

中国人的口味。在这场竞争中，中式、西式快餐可能
是双赢、多赢，而消费者将是最大的赢家。

Chinese and Western Fast Food Vie in China

Local and international companies are competing for shares in the fast food market in China. While McDonald's and Kentucky Fried Chickens are bourgeoning, various Chinese fast food and buffets also are attracting many diners. KFC has announced that it is committed to developing a new type of fast food adapted to the Chinese market. Before two Chinese fast food chains, Genuine Kungfu and Auntie's Dumplings entered the Beijing market, each had developed steadfast bases in southern Chinese cities such as Shanghai. Two local chains, Yonghe Soybean Milk and Malan Noodles have found overseas partners.

What is the future for fast food restaurants so busily gaining their footing in China? Statistics of the China Cuisine Association show that currently there are a million fast food outlets in China representing about 22% of restaurants, with annual revenue of 180 billion yuan. This is about 20% of the overall restaurant annual revenue. Each year, fast food chains account for one third of the top 100 restaurants in China. Analysts think that the quickening tempo of modern society will result in increasingly rapid growth.

However, in recent years there have been increasing numbers

of people becoming overweight and many nutritionists blame it on "foreign fast food culture". Some western fast food chains are frank that consumers' worries over the nutritional content of their food have begun to hinder their growth. Winning consumers' trust has become a compelling issue.

Chinese people have long advocated that a balanced intake of food is essential to health and are now requesting more balanced nutrition from the fast food industry. Chinese fast food chains are learning managerial experiences from their western counterparts, while the western ones are adapting to Chinese appetites and styles of local food. The competition of Chinese and Western fast food may be a win-win situation, with consumers as the best winners.

驰骋在高速公路上

一对中国夫妇在美国居住多年后，去年回到祖国，开始了他们的自驾车旅行。他们从北京走高速公路一路开到西安、成都，最后到达西藏。这样的旅行方式在他们刚离开中国的时候是不可想象的。因为中国那时还没有那么多顺畅的高速公路。现在，越来越多的中国人喜欢自己驾车在高速公路上。享受纵

情驰骋的快感，也可以沿途欣赏风光。

如今，从北京出发，你若去山东、辽宁、山西等周边各省，即使最远的地市，当天也可以往返，这在过去是难以想象的。因为这几个省都实现了省会到地市全部由高速公路连接，而长江三角洲、珠江三角洲、环渤海等经济发达地区的高速公路网络也正在形成。随着高速公路里程的不断延伸和规模效益的逐步发挥，中国人已切身感受到高速公路带来的时间、空间观念的变化。

中国大陆的第一条高速公路是1988年建成通车的，总长18.5公里，自上海至嘉定。此后不到20年时间，中国高速公路的总里程达到4.1万公里，位居世界第二位。2001年至2005年，高速公路快速发展，五年间建成高速公路2.47万公里，是前10年建成高速公路总里程的1.5倍。现在除西藏外，中国各省、自治区和直辖市都已拥有高速公路，有10个省份的高速公路里程超过1000公里。

据中国交通部的消息，中国今年还将斥资2万亿元，新建5.1万公里高速公路。到2030年，中国高速公路里程将达到8.5万公里，接近美国目前高速公路的长度。

Driving on the Expressway

A Chinese couple returned to their motherland last year, having lived in the US for many years. They undertook a journey by car on the expressways from Beijing to Xi'an and Chengdu, until finally they reached Tibet. Traveling in this way was unimaginable to them years ago when they left China, because there were no such unobstructed expressways in China in those days. At present, a significantly increasing number of Chinese people like to drive on the expressways, enjoying the pleasure from driving at will and enjoying the scenery along the road.

Today, when you leave Beijing for such neighboring provinces as Shandong, Liaoning and Shanxi, you can travel to and fro, even if you make your journey to a city comparatively far away from Beijing (an unthinkable feat in the past.) The aforementioned provinces have connected their provincial capitals and prefecture-level cities by expressways. The network of expressways in the Delta of the Yangtze River, the Delta of the Zhujiang River, and the economically developed areas around the perimeter of Bohai Bay is taking shape. With the seemingly unceasing stretch of expressways and the gradual achievement of mass efficacy, the Chinese people have experienced the temporal and spatial changes brought by the expressways.

The first expressway in China, 18.5 km long from Shanghai to Jiading, was open to traffic in 1988. In less than 20 years, the expressways in China have grown to 410,000 km, ranking second

in the world. From 2001 to 2005, the rapidly developing expressways increased by 24,700 km, 1.5 times as much as the total 10
years ago. Now, all provinces, autonomous regions and municipali-
ties directly under the Central Government of China, with Tibet
excluded, boast expressways, with 10 provinces exceeding 1,000 km
of expressway.

According to the Ministry of Communications, the Chinese
government will invest 2,000 billion yuan in construction of an
additional 51,000 km of expressways. In 2030, China will have a
total of 85,000 km of expressways, approximately equivalent to
the current total of expressways in the US.

养儿不再为防老

中国有句俗话：养儿防老。而今，这一延续了千百年的养老传统还灵验吗？

田德仁老人尽管还不到60岁，但视力不太好，听力也差，还有比较严重的糖尿病。今年初，他的女儿和女婿把他送进一家条件很好的民营敬老院。

同中国许多老人一样，田德仁心里很清楚，过去那种靠子女养老的传统，如今越来越不现实了。他唯一的女儿平时工作繁忙，经常要加班加点，他年幼的小外孙女还常常患病，需要女儿操心照料。女儿年迈的公婆也需要她抽时间看望和照顾。女儿在工作、家庭和父母之间来回奔波，的确有点力不从心。

相关统计数据显示，中国目前60岁以上的人口有1.44亿，占亚洲老年人口的一半，占全球老年人口的五分之一，中国成为世界老龄人口第一大国。这个数字每10年大约增长1亿。但在1000名老人中只有10张供他们所需要的养老床位，老年福利设施远远赶不上老年人数量的增长。

现在中国一般规定，男性退休年龄为60岁，女性为50岁或55岁，而许多公司迫使员工早点退休，让出职位留给年轻人。这些都令老年问题更为突出和恶化。

中国与一些经济发达国家不同，老年人的分布并不均匀，大多数老年人生活在较不富裕的农村地区，养老待遇和养老条件和城市相比更差些。

中国全国老龄工作委员会常务副主任李先生说，银发浪潮的快速袭来，给中国社会带来许多压力和问题。现在中国每三年就有300万人到了退休年龄，2006年中国有4600万离退休人员享受养老金，养老金支出已超过了5000亿元。老年人的医疗费用也在

成倍增加。农村的养老和医疗问题更为突出。到2030年后，将是中国老龄化的高峰时期，国家将面临一年1280亿美元的社会保障赤字。

面对银发浪潮，中国政府正在采取一些积极应对措施。比如，在城乡社区积极发展为老年人服务的产业，为他们提供生活照料、医疗保健、康复护理、家政服务、心理咨询、文化学习、体育健身、娱乐休闲等服务；对农村贫困老年人实行特殊社会救济和定期定量补助。国家财政也将逐步增加对老年服务设施、老年文化教育设施的投入，从福利彩票公益金中拨出一定比例用于老年服务事业，同时还鼓励民营资本和国外资本对此投入。

如今，中国人正从依靠子女养老向社会化养老转型，"养儿防老"的传统正在被打破。

Can We Raise Children Against Old Age

An old Chinese saying, "Raise children against old age" describes an old family custom of children providing assistance to their parents in their senior years. Can this long-standing tradition work well today?

Tian Deren, who is less than 60 years of age, has a poor eyesight and hearing, as well as serious diabetes. Early this year, his daughter and son-in-law sent him to a well-accommodated

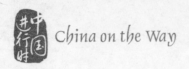

privately-operated house for the aged.

Like many old Chinese people, Tian Deren was clear that the old tradition of relying on children against old age was increasingly unrealistic. His only daughter is busy at work and often works overtime. Her daughter, who is very young, often falls ill and requires looking after, while her old parents-in-law also need her attendance. Constantly rushing about between her work, her family and her parents on both sides, she really feels worn out.

Statistics show that the older population at or over the age of 60 totals 144 million, accounting for half of that in Asia, or one fifth of that worldwide. Consequently, China has become the country with the largest senior population worldwide. This figure increases about 100 million every 10 years. But on the average, there is only room for about 1% of this number in homes for the aged. Such being the case, the welfare facilities for the old in China can hardly keep pace with the growth of its elderly population.

At present, it is generally provided in China that men and women retire at the age of 60 and 50 (or 55) respectively. A number of companies, however, encourage their employees to retire earlier, offering their positions to younger workers. This aggravates the problem facing seniors.

Unlike some economically developed countries, the elderly population in China is distributed unevenly. The older generations are more likely to live in rural poverty-stricken areas where treatment of the aged and general living conditions are worse than those

found in urban areas.

According to Mr. Li, managing vice-director of the China National Committee for the Aged, the wave of grey hair swiftly sweeping across the country exerts great pressure on China. Now, three million Chinese people reach the age of retirement every three years. The year 2006 witnessed 46 million Chinese retirees, whose pensions exceeded 500 billion yuan. Moreover, medical expenses for the aged grow at an alarming rate. Also, pressure is rising in the area of elder care. In particular, provisions for the aged and their medical care are of the greatest concern. Around the year 2030, China will reach a peak period of aging, with 128 billion US dollars of annual social security deficit facing the country.

Confronted with the sweeping wave of grey hair, the Chinese government is taking such positive countermeasures as actively developing industries related to serving the aged in rural and urban communities, and affording the aged daily attendance, medical and health care, recovery-oriented attendance, household management service, psychological consultation, elementary education, physical exercise, and entertainment. The aged poor in rural areas are given special social relief, as well as regular and fixed subsidies. The Chinese government will gradually invest more in service and educational facilities for the aged. In addition, a proportion of public welfare funds arising from welfare lottery tickets will be used to provide services for the aged, and the investment from privately-run and foreign enterprises is encouraged. As a result, caring for the aged is no longer merely a family responsibility, but more a social one.

留住眼前的美景

　　故宫、长城、黄山……中国这些世界知名的旅游景点每年都吸引着无数的中外游客前来观光。而随着中国列入"联合国世界文化与自然遗产"名录的景点的增多，再加上一些电影的拍摄与全球上映，许多原来并不知名的地方如今越来越受到人们的青睐。

　　安徽南部的宏村是一个典型的江南民居建筑的古村落，近年因其被申报为世界文化遗产项目，又因在此拍摄了影片《卧虎藏龙》，这个偏远的小村在海内外名声大振。现如今，一天有几千名游客涌入宏村旅游，感受影片中的美丽景致。

　　可宏村的村民们却发现，

他们昔日的宁静已渐渐远去，曾经清澈见底的溪水里，鱼儿正一天天减少……美国乔治·华盛顿大学旅游系主任于良教授对此指出，中国一些地方政府为了尽快致富，急于求成，过度利用当地旅游资源，推动经济发展。这不利于中国经济和旅游环境的良性发展。

中国各级政府也已经认识到，合理利用旅游资源和保护生态平衡对中国的长远发展具有同等的重要性，并已经着手采取相应的措施，例如九寨沟就已经实现现代化和电子化管理。中国政府已禁止那些以盈利为首要目的的公司参与管理自然文化遗产，并限制他们对一些文物古迹的盲目开发。目前，政府和许多专家学者正在研究既能保护自然与文化遗产，又能推动旅游事业发展的有效模式。相信经过努力，中国最终可以达到人与自然的和谐。

Save the Beautiful Sceneries Before Your Eyes

Every year, world-renowned places of interest in China such as the Palace Museum, the Great Wall, the Yellow Mountain, the Mountains and Waters of Guilin, etc. have attracted numerous Chinese and international tourists. As an increasing number of scenic locations in China have been recognized by the United Nations

World Cultural & Natural Heritage, along with the filming and the global staging of Chinese movies, many places which were previously unknown to most tourists are becoming more popular with people throughout the world.

The Hong Village in South Anhui Province is an ancient village with the typical architectural style found along the south of Yangtze River. In recent years, the small village, after being approved as a place of world cultural heritage and having been filmed in the famous movie *Crouching Tiger, Hidden Dragon*, is earning more and more reputation both at home and overseas. Nowadays, thousands of tourists flood to the Hong Village every day to experience and enjoy for themselves the beautiful scenery filmed in the movie.

However, the villagers had not expected their tranquility to abandon them with the increasing number of tourists. Nor had they anticipated the negative impact on the environment. Even the population of fish in the ever crystal brooks has dwindled… As for this phenomenon, Professor Liang Yu, Chair of the Department of Tourism at George Washington University in the United States, pointed out that some local governments in China disregard national interests, and are quick to exploit local tourism resources to promote local economic development in the short run. Naturally, they have paid no attention to sustainable development strategies and reasonable distribution of the local tourism resources, which has resulted in the dissatisfaction of the local people with the results.

Fortunately, Chinese government is becoming more and more

aware of the significance of some problems such as reasonable exploitation of tourism resources and responsible ecological protection. And the government has undertaken some corresponding measures. For example, the management of the Jiuzhaigou has become modernized and electronic. Currently, Chinese government has banned for-profit companies from participation in the management of natural and cultural heritages and it also has restricted random exploitation of ancient records and relics. At present, the government and resource management experts are endeavoring to locate an effective model, which can protect natural and cultural heritages and promote the tourism industry at the same time. It is firmly believed that with persistent efforts, China can achieve harmony between human beings and nature at long last, thus making a considerable contribution to the protection of the earth on which we live.

"扶贫"在行动

中国的人口约占世界总人口的22%,是世界上最大的发展中国家。在过去相当长的时间里,由于诸多原因,贫困一直困扰着中国。中国政府始终致力于解

决贫困人口的温饱问题，并有计划、有组织地实施大规模的扶贫开发，极大地缓解了贫困现象。从1978年到2005年，中国农村没有解决温饱问题的贫困人口由2.5亿人减少到2365万人，贫困人口占农村总人口的比例由30.7%下降到3%左右。在这些年间，各级政府为贫困地区兴修的基本农田达2688万亩，解决了7459万人的饮水困难。贫困村中，自然村通路、通电、通电话和通广播电视的比例达到71%、92.1%、49.1%和82.7%，使贫困地区的生产生活条件有了明显改善。世界银行前行长保罗·沃尔福威茨访问中国时曾说："中国的减贫成就举世瞩目。"

在中国，扶贫开发工作是由政府主导实施的，扶贫资金的投入也在逐年加大：2000年至2005年这五年间，中央财政扶贫开发资金累计投入572亿元，五年增长了36.8%，年均增幅达7.4%。地方财政累计投入170亿元左右。另外，农业、水利、教育、卫生、文化等部门在安排生产发展资金或社会发展资金时也向贫困地区有所倾斜。

中国的扶贫工作采取了各种途径和措施。其一，坚持开发式扶贫，强调扶贫到村到户，"小额信贷"就是实施开发扶贫到户的重要措施之一。其二，重视科技教育扶贫，在贫困地区引进推广农业科技成果，扶持发展特色农业，帮助贫困农民学习先进农业科技知识，改变贫困命运。此外，还开展了东部发达地区

支援西部贫困地区计划，实施了自然条件恶劣地区自愿移民的异地扶贫开发，以及支持开展贫困地区的劳务输出等。

近年来，一些非政府组织、私营企业和社会各界在扶贫中发挥的作用越来越大。他们举办了多种形式的扶贫活动，如帮助贫困地区小学生的"希望工程"、私营企业家支持贫困地区发展的"光彩事业"、帮助残疾人的"康复扶贫"、扶助贫困母亲的"幸福工程"、资助女童完成义务教育的"春蕾计划"、"青年志愿者支教扶贫接力计划"、"贫困农户自立工程"等。这些活动不仅取得了显著的扶贫成果，也产生了巨大的社会影响。

中国政府和人民创造的适合中国国情的扶贫模式，为提高扶贫资金的利用效率，加速减少贫困人口数量起到了积极作用。不少模式已成为世界扶贫事业中的典范，为其他国家提供了借鉴经验。

Aid-the-poor
Campaign Is Under Way

China, the population of which accounts for about 22% of that of the world, is the largest developing country in the world. Long ago, poverty was a constant plague in China for various reasons. The Chinese government has been devoting itself to assuring the

poor people's basic needs for food and clothing. A large-scale or-
ganized campaign to aid the poor has greatly alleviated their poverty.
From 1978 to 2005, those living without the basic necessities of
food and clothing in China's rural areas decreased from 250 million to 23.65 million, with the rate of the poor population dropping
from 30.7% to some 3% in the entire rural population. During these
years, Chinese governments at different levels established 26.88
million *mu* of basic farmlands in poverty-stricken areas, and also
provided drinking water for 74.59 million people. Many poverty-
stricken rural villages have built roads (71% nationally), established
electrical service (92.1%), telephone service (49.1%) and acquired
access to television and radio broadcasts (82.7%). As a result, the
conditions for production and life in these rural areas have appar-
ently improved. Paul Wolfowitz, former President of World Bank
said during his visit to China that China's achievements in alleviat-
ing poverty had attracted world attention.

In China, the aid-the-poor campaign was sponsored by the
government, and the investment in this program has been increasing annually. From 2000 to 2005, the Chinese Central Government's
investment in aid-the-poor project totaled 57.2 billion yuan, increasing by 36.8% in merely five years, or growing at an average annual
rate of 7.4%. Also, local governments made accumulative investments of 17 billion yuan for the aid-the-poor campaign. In addition,
departments of agriculture, water conservancy, education, public
health, culture and so on tilted in favor of the poverty-stricken areas in terms of the appropriation of the funds for productive and
social development.

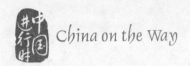

China has taken various measures in the aid-the-poor work. First, the Chinese government adheres to exploitation-oriented assistance to the poor by stressing the aid to the poor from village to village and from household to household. The "small-sum credit" granted to households is an important measure to practice the aid-the-poor program. Second, the Chinese government attaches importance to providing scientific technology assistance to the poor. The program introduces advanced agricultural achievements to poverty-stricken areas, renders support for the development of key agricultural products, and extends assistance to poor farmers in their study of advanced agricultural knowledge to assist them in their pursuit of a change in their destiny. Other elements of the aid-the-poor program include encouragement by the government to have developed areas in Eastern China render assistance to the poverty-stricken areas in Western China, a voluntary relocation project for those living in adverse natural conditions, and labor assistance for poverty-stricken areas.

In recent years, some non-governmental organizations, privately-run enterprises and people from all walks of life have been playing an increasingly significant role in the aid to the poor. They have performed various aid-the-poor activities, such as the "Hope Project" aimed at helping primary school students in poverty-stricken areas, the "Honorable Cause" founded by entrepreneurs from privately-run enterprises who assist in the development of poverty-stricken areas, the "Recovery-oriented Assistance to the Poor" to help the disabled, the "Happiness Project" to assist poor mothers, the "Spring-bud Plan" to subsidize poor girls' completion of compulsory education, the "Plan for Young Volunteers to Support Teaching

in Poverty-stricken Areas by Relays", and the "Poor Farmers' Self-supporting Project", all of which have achieved outstanding results and produced an enormous social improvement.

The Chinese government and its people have created aid-the-poor patterns appropriate to China's national conditions, and have proven to be efficient in the utilization of the aid-the-poor funds and have rapidly reduced the poor population. Many of those patterns have become classical cases worldwide for other countries to use for reference.

游走在都市的乞讨者

走在中国上海的繁华大街上，你几乎感觉有梦一般的色彩。中午时分的南京路上，发型优美、衣着得体的行人会让你赏心悦目，尤其是二三十岁的女性，她们对时尚的准确把握丝毫不输于日本东京的女人。

无论哪个周末，你来到上海的购物街——淮海路，这里的景象更加引人注目。也许时尚气息没那么明显，但在熙熙攘攘的人群中，你常常可以看到大肆购物后的人们，那种满足感仍停留在他们的脸上，尽管中国人以爱攒钱著称。

但是，如果你留心的话，在南京路和淮海路上众多新富行人的掩映当中，你也可以看到衣衫褴褛者靠捡垃圾箱里的废物为生，弯腰驼背、满脸皱纹的老人在街角乞求救济……

其实，城市流浪乞讨是世界各国普遍存在的现象，中国也不例外。这些城市乞讨者的存在原因也

是多方面的，既有贫困的原因，也有个别生活方式选择的原因。中国政府一直坚持对这个特殊群体给予引导与关心，相关机构也对他们进行人性化的管理救助。

随着中国社会各方面体系不断完善，涵盖面广、有效的社会救助系统逐步形成，城市乞讨者是否会越来越少呢？我们拭目以待。

Beggars Roaming the Metropolis

Walking on some streets in Shanghai can almost give you a dreamlike feeling. If you happen to walk on the Nanjing Road at noon, you will be delighted by the sight of passers by with pleasant hairstyles and elegant clothes, especially those women in their twenties or thirties. They are capable of catching the latest fashion as accurately as the ladies of Tokyo, Japan.

On any weekend, if you go to the Huaihai Road — the second most famous shopping street in Shanghai, you will find an even more fascinating scene. Although it may appear less fashionable, among the crowds, you will still find people wearing satisfied smiles after a crazy day of shopping, despite the Chinese tradition of saving money.

However, if you pay enough attention, you will also note among the crowds of the rich on the Nanjing Road, people with

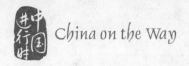

ragged clothes making a living by picking garbage from the trashcans and old people with hunched backs and wrinkled faces begging on the corner.

As a matter of fact, wanderers and beggars are a common sight in cities of all countries throughout the world, and China is no exception. It seems that the reasons for this are varied and manifold, including, among other things, poverty, and the personal life style choices. Regardless of the reasons for their condition, these people should have their own room to survive. The Chinese government has provided positive instruction and delicate care for this special group of people, has also provided some humanitarian arrangements and assistance. With constant improvement of every aspect of society and the gradual establishment of a comprehensive and effective social relief system, will the numbers of beggars in the cities be reduced? Let's wait and see.

大学生
从"精英"走向"大众"

　　26岁的化学专业毕业生余梦坐了20个小时的火车，从偏远的甘肃省来到北京参加招聘会。在人头攒动的招聘摊位前，手执简历的她努力地向前走着。

余梦的周围是来自全国各地的数千名将要毕业和已经毕业的高校学生，大家都在为了能找到一个较为满意的工作岗位而奔波忙碌。而实现这个梦想对现在的大学毕业生们并非易事。

过去30年中国大学毕业生的就业状况表明，大学生正经历着从"精英"走向"大众"的转变。自从1977年中国恢复高考制度后，80年代初中期的大学生分配去向非常不错，许多国家党政机关、事业单位都到各大院校"抢"毕业生；而后，随着国家高等教育的改革，大学毕业不再由国家分配，毕业生开始自谋职业。自90年代末以来，各大学连年扩大招生，高等教育规模不断扩大。现在每年大学毕业生人数至少是10年前的4倍。

高等教育的日渐普及化，势必给大学生就业带来一些新问题，这需要政府、社会、高等院校、用人单位和大学毕业生等几方面的统筹解决和合力应对。

我们已经看到，政府有关部门针对大学生就业的难点热点，出台和调整了一些政策条令，为大学生顺利就业和发挥才干创造良好环境。社会各部门广开渠道，举办各种人才招聘会，为大学生求职排忧解难。还有许多用人单位和培训机构针对社会需求对大学生进行就业再培训，以提高他们适应社会竞争的能力。

大学毕业生们也在逐步转变就业观念，千方百

计提高个人素质和能力，去迎接各种挑战。

Job-hunting University Students

It took Yu Meng, a 26-year-old university graduate majoring in chemistry, 20 hours traveling by train to Beijing for a talent fair sponsored by the remote province of Gansu. In front of the crowded employee-recruiting stand, she struggled to step forward, with her curriculum vitae in hand. Around Yu Meng were thousands of students having recently completed their studies, or soon to graduate from universities around the country. They were each seeking a satisfactory job, a dream difficult for them to come true.

The employment of Chinese university graduates in the past three decades has transitioned from selecting students who represented the elite of contemporary youth to those representing the common people. After the system of the university entrance examination was resumed in China in 1977, university students who graduated in the beginning and middle of the 1980s were assigned to decent jobs as large numbers of government organizations and public institutions rushed to colleges and universities to recruit their graduates. Afterwards, with the reform of higher education in China, university graduates, instead of being assigned jobs by the state, started seeking jobs for themselves. Since the end of the 1990s, China's colleges and universities have increased their enrollment of students annually leading to the continuous growth of university graduates. Now, the annual number of university graduates is at least four times that of a decade ago.

The gradual popularization of higher education is sure to bring about new problems pertaining to the employment of university graduates, which must be tackled in a coordinated manner with concerted efforts by the government, social groups, institutions of higher learning, employee-recruiting units, and university graduates.

We have seen that relevant departments of the Chinese government, considering the difficult points involving the employment of university graduates, have formulated and adjusted some policies and regulations so as to create a better environment for university graduates to successfully find employment and give full play to their talents. Concerned social agencies tap all channels available and hold various talent fairs to help university graduates solve their job-seeking difficulties. Furthermore, many employee-recruiting units and training agencies, according to social demands, offer university graduates employment-related re-training in order to enhance their social adaptability and competitiveness.

University graduates are gradually changing their concept of employment, and are trying every means to raise their personal quality and capability to adapt themselves to society.

责任编辑：翟淑蓉

英文编辑：郭　辉

封面设计：古　手

印刷监制：佟汉冬

图书在版编目（CIP）数据

中国进行时：汉英对照／刘东平编.—北京：华语教学出版社，2007
（我的第一本中国读物）

ISBN 978-7-80200-389-7

I. 中… II. 刘… III. ①汉语－对外汉语教学－语言读物②中国－概况－
英、汉 IV. H195.4 K92

中国版本图书馆 CIP 数据核字（2007）第 175165 号

中国进行时

刘东平　翟淑蓉　编著

*

© 华语教学出版社出版

（中国北京百万庄大街 24 号　邮政编码 100037）

电话：(86)10-68320585

传真：(86)10-68326333

网址：www.sinolingua.com.cn

电子信箱：hyjx@sinolingua.com.cn

北京外文印刷厂印刷

中国国际图书贸易总公司海外发行

（中国北京车公庄西路 35 号）

北京邮政信箱第 399 号　邮政编码 100044

新华书店国内发行

2007 年（16 开）第一版

2008 年第一版第二次印刷

（汉英）

ISBN 978-7-80200-389-7

9-CE-3856P

定价：38.80 元